I0758732

Unapologetically Black
Shamira Camper

Table of Contents

This book is dedicated to every victim who lost their lives due to senseless acts of hatred and violence.

Introduction
"Our Lives Matter"

They say all lives matter, but you're exempt, not included, it seems when your skin color is black.

They say we're all supposed to be treated equally, yet all the minorities and people of color are continually being killed or brutally attacked.

They say they plan to seek justice for all, but if they had any consideration, remorse, or empathy, they wouldn't have done half the stuff they've done like taking the life of an innocent kid.

They say it's not only people of color being shot down in the streets like dogs leaking from several shots to their bodies or head.

They say we all exaggerate. We go out of our way to fabricate stories. Yet, why is it that every time we turn around, they're filling one of our unarmed loved ones up with large amounts of lead?
They say every life is important, regardless of your choice of religion, financial status, attire, residence, or your nationality.

They say that Abraham Lincoln signing that declaration made a huge difference; supposedly that emancipation made every one of every race equal, it made even all of us blacks free.

They say Big Mike, Young Trayvon, Alton Sterling, Philando Castile, Oscar Grant, Eric Garner, Terence Crutcher, and Lamont Scott were all being aggressive, acting suspicious, refusing to obey their commands, attempting to flee the scene, or carrying a gun.
 They fed the media, us the people, and their fellow officers who aren't corrupt, a bunch of bullshit. They've made way too many excuses for their unjust actions, but when it came time actually to present a real case or weapon, there wasn't one.

They say the pigs wearing black or blue, I mean the cops, are not suspects or criminals. The cops are nothing more than our personal heroes, they sacrifice their lives daily to protect and serve, but they break more laws than all the part-time crooks and so-called thugs. Some police officers and politicians often move sneakily behind the public's watching and wandering eye. They commit all sorts of crimes from extortion, rape, robbery, sex trafficking, drugs, and other kinds of unlawful acts of dirt.

They say the lives of law enforcement, political officials, Donald Trump, and other people who have white skin should matter just as much. However, they're the main reason why the world is divided, chaotic, and in turmoil. They're the reason us blacks are upset, rioting, acting out, protesting, distraught, grieving, angry, and full of unbearable pain that hurt.

They say we pose a great threat; then, we play the victim as if we're not out here recklessly shooting our own kids during gang wars that transpire daily. We're savages as well who look forward to killing each other.

They say California, Chicago, and Baltimore are the cities of drugs and death. We don't want much out of life, and none of us really care for ourselves, so how are we any different if we kill our own sisters, friends, and brother?

They say we deserve to be caged or shot down. Over one hundred and fifty people have been killed this year with ease because we're just a bunch of thugs, a race that acts like wild animals or a group of individuals who're simply unfit.

They say welfare, medicine, Medicaid, and food stamps should be taken away along with other resources many folks reach out to in their time of need. We always want something for free, they say. They also say we're just a bunch of lazy, ignorant, niggers who they feel aren't worth shit.

They say the judicial system was made to make sure justice would prevail before an innocent person is slain or convicted on false charges. However, freedom, most times, is granted to the opposition only. In return, many believe that they are invincible or above the law.

They say, George Zimmerman, the racist punk, was right for assaulting and killing an unarmed teen. The state of Florida called it standing his ground. He wasn't found guilty, nor has anyone else been held accountable for contributing to the deaths of so many innocent folks. They're quick to prejudge, tell lies, or pretend, knowing all along their true intentions were to shoot on sight. Truth is they were hoping to see another one of our black asses nobody cares about will drop, bleed out, and fall.

They say, along with the NRA, that our children, brothers, sisters, cousins, nieces, aunts, uncles, and parents all deserved what their narrow black asses got.

They say our daughters aren't worth much. They deserve to be killed in prison or kidnapped, drugged, abused, and sold. They claim if the victims weren't acting so "thirsty" or too combative, they wouldn't have come up missing or found themselves being another victim of the American tradition. They say the color of our skin made us guilty; we needed to be shot.

They say us bastards have let money, addiction, and freedom go to our heads. We must have forgotten where we came from and had we still been the slaves we were born to be; we wouldn't have gotten so out of hand. They say we're wrong for reacting, wanting better, and for not bowing down to white power, our primary opposition. They say we're in the wrong period for fighting back also for finally taking a stand.

They say they aren't the real enemy, more so victims. However, each time the news comes on, they've just shot or killed another black kid, woman, or man.

They say we won't make it; we can't and will never change what's always been, "The American Way." They say we have to settle for less because we have no other choice. I beg to differ; I say we can make it happen if we try harder, think smarter, and stick together as an unbreakable force with a powerful voice.

They have done and said a lot. Fuck what they say. We're tired of the mistreatment, separation, and humiliation; it isn't just the drugs and guns they sold us that have destroyed our communities, torn our families, and distorted our brains.

They say we've grown accustomed to ignorance our negative reactions prove we will never change. Again, fuck what they say. We're frustrated and overwhelmed so we're just not taking their bullshit anymore. We're beyond tired. We're fed up we're not going back to ropes, whips, fields, outhouses, sugar shacks, and chains.

Chapter One

"Dirty Cops"
They're Breaking the Law So; We Say Fuck Them All...

The buses, subways, and light rails unloaded fast. Everyone is in a hurry and anxious to meet up directly after all the schools were dismissed. The plan had been set in motion, and social media was used to make the mission go viral. People wasted no time getting down to business. Some people were moving so quickly that a few were knocked down and trampled over. Corner stores, bars, pharmacies, and the malls were being robbed. I saw folks stealing televisions, clothing, shoes, and more. The dope fiends and junkies had a ball. They took all they could take, then took a break to shoot up in the bathroom stall. Today, everyone is on their best bullshit. They were feeling themselves and not giving two fucks about anything, especially the law. Traffic was abruptly brought to a halt and eventually completely stopped.

The pharmacy was raided; they stole all the pills they could take. It seemed the entire world was strung out or addicted to some sort of prescription pill. I guess nobody thought about the granny who was on the way to pick up her medication to take when she ate her next meal. That shit was dumb and served no purpose; I will be the first to say it. While some flocked to the church for help and prayer, the rest flocked to the streets where they could confront the corrupt police. Glass bottles were thrown, and stop signs were torn down or covered with graffiti.

The buildings and different types of public establishments were set ablaze, and cars were stolen, vandalized, and destroyed. Nobody could get the situation under control. Most people were too angry, and the rest were too afraid. From the outside looking in, it's as if the city of Baltimore had lost its mind. The truth is, the events of that evening and other events around the world have left too many people scarred, dead, starving, imprisoned, and forgotten. They felt it was necessary, or they wouldn't have been able to obtain results in any other way. Store owners and rich white folks are extremely terrified that they may be robbed or the next victim of a senseless homicide. The oppressor says the color of our skin is a weapon. They can use that weapon to divide us and create weaknesses. However, if we united and started being who we were created to be, there wouldn't be a chance in hell they could defeat or stop us. They've instilled fear and created foundations based on the hate they gave us. They gave us every tool we would need to destroy ourselves with death, bondage, and division. This has always been the American way. Their hatred wasn't just given to the infants, as the Legend Tupac said it fucked us all. He spoke on these current events years ago, and they called him crazy, troublesome, and a thug. Everything Tupac said fit tighter than O.J. Simpson's glove. Now they're scared, now they have complaints, now we're the aggressor with no restraints, and now they want to call the law. They can't walk one day in our shoes. How dare they have the audacity to complain when they have spent decades using us treating us worst? I can see what instilled the most fear: us standing together as one gives us strength in numbers. That day, shit got real, and I have no empathy because for once, they get to see how being mistreated hasn't been easy to endure. It was like back in the 1950's block to block a massive group of angry people ready to go to war with the cops. Mothers worried about their kids: they don't know if they were headed home or on the avenue possibly out there speaking their peace or acting a fool. Some parents approved it; others were prepared to bust ass and drag their kids home, embarrassing them if they had to in the process. They were doing it out of love and protecting their lives because they didn't understand how dangerous the situation was and how they could get hurt or killed. They were standing up for their beliefs, for our rights, or just trying to protest. What they don't understand is that the color of their skin puts them at a high risk of being shot for less.

Buildings were set ablaze, rival gangs united and came together for the cause as if they aren't here killing just as many if not more than the law. I wasn't impressed by that. Killing each other isn't cool, especially when all our skin color is black. They are no better than the corrupt officers. The world needs more love and understanding. We've been denied, ignored, overlooked, and forgotten for so long that some of us can't resist being overly aggressive and extremely demanding.

 The teens and some adults have decided to bring the battle to their front doors. We're not afraid anymore. We have artillery as well, thanks to them shipping in guns galore. Many have never left the city, let alone the state, yet they own AK 47's from Russia. We hold all types of firearms that should've never come, but the government and Jim Crow wanted to divide conquer and wipe us out so we would end up like the Native Americans. When you count how many are left compared to the rest, there's none. I guess that's why the city was loaded with aggression, tension, and all sorts of weapons, including a gun. I don't condone every action that we saw that day, but I do entirely understand their pain and do agree to a certain extent in a nonviolent way like Martin Luther King Jr. Don't get me wrong, Malcolm X and the black panther motto by any means necessary also brought forth results.

 It just sometimes made the task more difficult at hand, but when is it easy when we're dealing with the white man. I had never seen a cop or cracker move so fast as they did when a mob of kids came prepared to fight, putting a much-needed foot up their ass. The streets got flooded quickly with a bunch of angry black folk who'd become fed up carrying broken bottles, machetes, rocks, pipes, wooden boards, baseball bats, cocktail bombs, sticks, and broken pieces of glass. Our anxiety level grew high, and our patience ran out. I heard some popped a few Percocet's, Zanies', Adderall, and molly. They said it was their way of getting war-ready. They were numbing the pain, and they wanted to make sure they felt nothing or feared nobody when it was time to battle on the frontline. When some individuals are intoxicated, it gives them an extra cape of strength and the ability to walk around with their chest poked out. Duress, denial, and unlawful deaths caused people to snap resorting to a dangerous point of no return, no surrender, no retreat, and no clearing out the city streets. Most days, when law enforcement came in large packs like big hungry alley rats, the average person would scatter but not today. To their surprise, we refused to be walked over, ignored, or moved. We've lost too many innocent young and older people. We've been mistreated. We can no longer withstand the storm; it has been raining way too long we need them to feel and to hear us loud and clear. It hasn't been enough just praying for change to come. Look how long ago it was when Sam Cooke sang that classic song and look how much more we've endured since then. We took all we could and lost many.

They said they couldn't take any more of the nonsense and were all tired of it. In every way possible, we 've been screwed over, taken advantage of, deprived, starved, fed drugs, and imprisoned for ridiculous amounts of years for something minor. Most of the kids we see today have fathers who are incarcerated, single mothers; both parents are addicted or being raised by grandparents who are too old to be efficient. Everyone seems to be out of control. A lot of the "so-called" leaders of the block or communities that many of the youth look up to or follow behind weren't leading in the right direction with such a negative example of how to obtain justice or the right to be heard in general. Several known associates of Mr. Gray have been put under illegal surveillance, harassed, stalked, locked up, lied on, families threatened, freedom taken away, jeopardized their rights, or was taken to discreet locations then slaughtered. True justice has yet to be granted, but evidence has been hidden or concealed, and numerous money transactions have been revealed. Fraudulent statements are given and seeds of hatred have been planted. The cops are still free, no arrests have been made. Freddie's family is mourning with no answers. We can't take any more of the brutality by officers of the law who are never convicted but lie and plant evidence on the crime scenes contaminating everything as they did with the case of the young girl allegedly found dead in a freezer named Kenneka. We bury loved one after a loved one, are given high bails we can't pay and are being falsely accused. That's how Kalief Browder's life ended up slipping away along with his mother. The system failed the Browder family; it failed us, black people. Now they're mad because some of us have chosen to take a stand against the man and fight back. So many have been imprisoned or murdered for no reason other than the color of their skin. If they were white, especially rich, powerful, stuff like this wouldn't be. Their family businesses, neighborhoods, and homes aren't being burned to the ground. They're killing Mike Trey and Sandy, but they're not bothering Sue, who can take lives. They're not coming for Tommy; he has mental issues, so his actions should be excused. He doesn't need to be in prison; he needs to be in a hospital receiving proper treatment. Tommy and Bobby need help.

They're the real victims, not the cold, corpse laid out in the bushes, car, prison, or cement. They've done so much wrong and have rarely ever been charged despite how many have been killed worldwide. They laugh at our pain like it's a joke, just like they did with Eric Garner when he was choked. Those officers were never charged or convicted, and his daughter Ericka suffered a massive heart attack and died as a result. Trayvon and his parents' character were demeaned by Zimmerman and everyone in the courtroom, including his team. They pretended he was a saint and that he could never do such a thing, but as soon as the trial was over, a lot of his little lying hummingbirds started to sing. They thought the shit was funny and hid valuable evidence. They turned the entire case into a circus act because they had no respect, consideration, or empathy for those who sat most days in tears, outraged that their son, nephew, or brother was never coming back. George, the obsessed heartless jerk, has fooled many just like Satan himself.

Those who supported the ignorant, racist, prick is also the devil's advocate. They didn't let anyone speak for Trayvon, not his brothers or parents who would've gladly spoken in his honor, not just his defense. Due to neglect, poor judgment, and the truth being concealed, those dumbfounded jurors were left in suspense. They had long ago formed an opinion about the young man way before they were even asked for their two cents. Civil rights lawyer Benjamin Crump who first represented the Martin family, was thrown off the case and ejected from the courtroom at times, but the same man that defamed their character, I mean deposed of all the witnesses, was the same person to defend the suspect accused of murder. Nobody who would've and wanted to protect him was allowed, but the defense pretty much did whatever they wanted without any objection or interruption from the prosecution. They didn't bother to cross-examine, and the defense attorneys were going out their way to make a mockery of the situation. They were making sure to pull out all their stunts, assumptions, and fronts giving the already tainted and biased jurors precisely what he knew they would want. Since then, the racist asshole who got away with cold-blooded murder has obtained six different mugshots or more after being arrested for several things like domestic violence and assault with deadly weapons. They continue to let him threaten or wave that gun at whoever; girlfriends, exes, black teenagers, and all but wasn't charged. He has been charged with aggravated assault, threatening to kill a motorist pointing a gun at the same lying bitch who he had get on the stand and lie she also did lots of dirty work for and with him. He's turned into an arrogant psychopath taunting the Martin and Fulton family, our race, and all of us as a whole. He's gone nuts, and he just has no control or limits to what he will do. That's because the sorry ass system that's supposed to protect us and our rights refused used the case for political gain, money, and positions of power. They ignored our call for help and justice again and didn't come through. Instead, he's been treated like some sort of celebrity: his kind is proud of him. They not only support and encourage the heartless jerk, but they also contribute to his ignorance and finances as well. They all deserve a permanent seat in hell. It's disgusting to see how we've been treated everything is being recorded live put on the internet social media outlets or televised and still that holds no power to change everything no one cares or has replied to our cries.

He's been sponsored by the NRA, KKK, other white racists, and so many more. Still, yet he was found not guilty just like all the rest who got away with murder and Trayvon was demeaned, stereotyped and profiled by a civilian who decided to take the law into his own hands after prejudging the young man just for being black and wearing a hoodie. He was unmercifully killed and was labeled as a thug. Since his death, we have stood united, supporting the Black Lives Matter movement. Many celebrities are showing support and love in hopes that justice may one day be served and that people will never forget the tragic unlawful murder he claims was an accident or self-defense. They're killing our children which has become a trend not much has changed since that Declaration of Emancipation was signed. What happened to him and many others are the sad history of our people and so-called civil rights. They're killing our kids, which isn't new; look at what they put Mrs. Mamie Till through. I shed tears for them all. My heart goes out to Sabrina Fulton, Tracy Martin, and all the many other parents who're left grieving over the loss of an innocent child. They criticize and prosecute us for any and everything, but they're breaking the law without the worry or fear of consequences. They're quick to prejudge us but have no problem doing dirt. They're making false arrests, extorting drug dealers, raping females, killing kids, and enjoying causing senseless fatalities. In the war, of course, there's always unfortunate casualties that's to be expected, but we're not on a battlefield somewhere in Kuwait or Iraq. It may seem that way because almost daily, there's blood being shed, and nine times out of ten, it's a colored Islamic or Hispanic individual covered in white sheets laid out dead. Now they're crying victim because the rabbit now has the gun it's no longer funny cause we have the upper hand. What goes around comes around as Zimmerman said the frustrated youth was a threat: he was black and suspicious, and concrete was his weapon, he was defenseless and allegedly was just standing his ground. The state of Florida says he was just merely protecting their families and guarding their homes. Now, the tables have turned, and the fact that they're eager to rock one of those white men in blue into a permanent sleep got us looking like a pack of hungry wolves and them the weak, innocent flock of sheep. We've instantly become the aggressors again, which is always easy in a world where we're the black sheep. Today was beyond crazy it was like the riot in Watts LA, back in the day when they beat Rodney King for not a damn thing. Or in Ferguson after the death of an innocent young black man named Mike Brown. That's another reason so many were out there showing their natural black asses as the opposition called it. They were being shot down like wild dogs. We wanted answers, and we wanted the judicial system to fight for us as they do for their own. The point was to seek justice for Freddie and all the others who lost their lives to senseless violence due to the hands of law enforcement.

Of course, the news was going to show all the negatives that didn't make a difference or a positive impact. I'm pissed off too, but sometimes we have to be more cautious in the way we think, move and react. They wait for us to slip or for a so-called reason to pull out a pistol quickly, pulling the trigger saying our reckless behavior causes a chain reaction that was bound to counteract. We were already walking targets and have never been given any slack. They rejoice each time they make us look bad, blaming it on our lack of education, laziness, drug usage, or parents. Fox and CNN tried to go out their way to make us all look ignorant, ignoring the real task at hand. It was never about money, looting, being violent, or being on camera trying to get our little five minutes of fame. We came together to protest, to stand our ground, to be heard loud in clear without showing an ounce of fear though we did end up whipping a few of them severely while shedding many tears. We cried for those who lost their lives. We cried because nothing has been done to any of the suspects. My heart nearly stopped when I saw little Tamir Rice who'd been playing with toys guns with a friend at the park on a cold winter day get so much lead fired into his small, frail chest that was only covered with a coat unlike them who had real weapons and a vest.

I'm Teflon tough, but when I saw his body shake, then eventually drop, I cried. I felt hatred towards all the cops and people like the old boy from down south. George Zimmerman is still walking around like a neighborhood hero but really a lying jerk loser straight-up zero. Things need to be addressed differently than the way it's always been. For years now, we have been running this race, and we 've had enough. To have something so tragic happen added a lot of fuel to the engulfing fire. If justice had been served, the show out in North Carolina and Ferguson might have never been. They didn't send in the national guard when the KKK and tons of other whites stormed the streets armed and dangerous down in Charlottesville, Virginia or when they were draped down in their torn white dingy sheets. Due to all the tension, our roads were crowded earlier with bricks, gas jugs, baseball bats, pistols, handguns, and rifles. They were fully equipped with ammunition. Grandma at home is praying in the kitchen after humming her favorite gospel hymn while frying her famous chicken unaware that her granddaughter was headed down the block with the rest of the angry, frustrated teenagers on a dangerous mission. Terry crying because Freddie Gray was her cousin, the innocent man was killed. News reporters say we were going wild and they called them everything but somebody's child. The streets are crowded; the smoke is thick. We're out here on Penn & North Avenue throwing bricks because we're sick of this shit. Things didn't have to come to this, but the sorry ass government refuses to handle it. They don't care about us or the way the dirty cops are shooting us down. They label us as the thugs and killers, but the real gangsters are being exposed now, and nothing is being done about the troubling issue in DC or downtown. The people have grown tired of waiting for their so-called help.

 They've begun to protect and serve themselves. They've lost faith in the system and trust in them. I don't blame them either, especially after what they've done to so many of our kin. I believe they enjoy seeing us trying to defeat the struggle. Why do you think they've secluded most of us to the projects, public housing, and other areas of the jungle? The plan has always been to keep us in the middle to suffer, to do their dirty work, and to destroy one another. They try to be slick, but we all know what happens when you're put in the ring under pressure. They set us up for failure the day we were declared free, and they've just been sitting back waiting for us to fumble. They want us to kill each other; that's why they flood our communities with guns from Russia and other foreign soils. They want drugs to be sold to our mothers, so they ship drugs from Colombia, Afghanistan, Amsterdam, and Bangkok. They don't want our kids to succeed. They want us to lose our sons, uncles, nephews, and brothers. That's why the officers keep leaving blood trails behind using white sheets on their dead bodies for a cover. They strive to build an atmosphere where we will continue to go against one another or fail, and some of us are giving them exactly what they want to no avail. Many don't have any other choice because they're constantly being ignored, overlooked, or imprisoned. Having few options to survive has provoked them to make bad decisions. Changes need to be made, but their cries and all of our pain is being brushed off or denied. I'm writing this book to give them a voice. I'm tired of my people being unheard of. I want to help them get the chance that they deserve personally. It's time for everybody to sit their ass down and listen. I mean damn, how many more kids have to come up dead or missing for them to finally take a look at the bigger picture? My people and I are hurting bad and whether they want to acknowledge the problem or not, us blacks are under attack. It's as if somebody marked an x on our back demanding we be slaughtered, and they aren't cutting us any slack. We're being killed by dirty cops and the white man in huge numbers. It's ridiculous how many fucking lives were taken away this summer. Not to mention the 102 unarmed black people who were killed during the year 2015. Out of the 12 cases, only 10 of them resulted in charges. One hundred thirty-six black people have been killed thus far in this current year of 2016 (Sad Truth), and it's not even over yet. Unarmed blacks are more likely than whites to be killed by police officers. Just like most of the blacks here in the city are more likely to go to jail than to a university, this is a known fact. In my eyes, something is seriously wrong with that. We need to take control of our lives back. I'm tired of police brutality. I can only imagine how many more lives will be lost, and at what cost? Where's the justice at?

To make matters worse than what they already are, we're also out here acting like damn fools killing each other. I've lost so many friends and family members to a gang and gun violence or drugs that I've honestly been unable to keep count. I'm sick of this shit. If they kill us and we continue to do the same, the end results will be very harsh but a reality. We would no longer exist. That frightens me, and I don't want stuff to continue on like this.

I know our ancestors and descendants are disappointed. I see more dead bodies surfacing on the news than I do a new music video, movie, or cartoon. A lot of people believe they're above the law just like the former police officer Michael Dowd, a self-made gangster in New York from the 75th precinct and many other of his crooked fellow officers around the world. They're all corrupt as shit still to this day. They prey on the weak and the less fortunate. They refuse to make a change. They refuse to take responsibility for their fucked-up actions, and their reckless behavior displays that. They're killing innocent people pretending to have been under attack or reaching for a Taser gun as if they haven't received the proper training in police tactics. Those cops are full of it. They just don't care, and they've got the potential to take a life anywhere. We don't have any safe zones anymore; they're killing us everywhere, including in broad daylight, in a compacted space, in a car, or a crowded store. It disgusts me how the pigs take advantage of their position and us all whenever and in any way that they can. The officers of the law who took the same oath as the president will gun you down quicker than they do a duck. They treat our family members as their personal prey, and they're thirsty for our blood. The stuff they do to us is foul. They've made it very clear that they just don't give a fuck. They kill with no remorse what so ever. They're not just abusing us; they're also taking advantage of their position of power. They may have destroyed a lot of evidence of J. Edgar Hoover and others who did dirt, but that changes nothing. Not much has changed, but the date, us blacks still have a lot piled up on our plates. I've seen them planting drugs on minors, soliciting women for sex, and staging false murders.

They pretend the victims were all carrying or reaching for some sort of weapon. Their favorite lie is a gun. The other excuse is we act combative, too aggressive, our skin is too dark, or we wore a hoodie or other attire they don't approve of. Let them tell it; they'll say young Trayvon and the rest of those who were murdered were posing a serious threat. It's a lot of excuses being made, but the reality is we're tired, and we are not giving in or up. We've gained the courage of some of our ancestors and started fighting back. I respect Dr. King's nonviolent movement. I appreciate what he and many others did who fought hard and lost their lives for our rights and all but fuck that. They out this bitch buying ass, telling lies, killing innocent men, women, and children, and getting away with it.

Something needs to be done, but this may not have been the best or exact way to go about handling such a deadly but already fragile situation. Because of their little metal badge, they act as if they've been given the privilege to do whatever the hell they want. They feel they are above us. They feel our lives aren't worth much. They think they're invincible. Nah scratch that, untouchable. They really believe the senseless murders being committed is cool. They enjoy harassing us in the streets or locking our children up at school.

Those bastards are hurting our babies for fun. They're shooting us down like it's a sport, and help from the government is never found when we need support. I'm tired of us being the ones to come up short. Where the hell is the justice at? Tamir Rice, Tarnisha Anderson, Tiara Thomas, Alton Sterling, Philando Castile, Eric Garner, Rekia Boyd, Bettie Jones, Chandra Weaver, Aiyahna Stanley-Jones, Kendra James, Nicholas Thomas, Eric Harris, Kevin Matthews, Alonzo Smith, Oscar Grant, Christopher Kimble, Yvette Smith, Keith McLeod, India Kayer, Asshams Manley, Spencer McCain, Darnisha Harris, Miriam Carey, Matthew Ajibade, Keith Childress and Patterson Brown. The list of names could go on and on forever. I pray for all the families who lost loved ones to senseless bullshit. I pray for the victims who've now moved on way too soon; may their souls rest in peace. I ask you once again, where justice for those people is? Where's the justice for the rest of the folks still living who are hurting and grieving?

Where's the justice for my race? Where's the justice for being me? Every day the crooked crackers (and pigs of color too) are out roaming the streets and highways laying somebody out on their stomach or back. God bless America. God bless the trap. God bless the minorities. God bless our children. God bless other countries. God bless us, blacks. Out of all the classes of people to flex on, they unleash their hatred and ignorant ways upon us colored folks the most. 90% of mass shootings have been by the hands of white people, but I've never heard anyone refer to them as thugs, savages, or terrorists. Don't get me wrong; a few whites have suffered police brutality as well, but the murder and injustice rate that they have afflicted upon us people of color don't come close. Unarmed blacks are fourteen times more likely to be killed by the police than whites. They treat us unfairly, acting as if we have no rights. During the current year of two thousand and something, there's still no equality for us all.

Damn shame. Just eight years ago when President Barack Obama was elected, we were celebrating, full of cheer, out in the streets of Washington DC all the way down to the deep country back roads of southern states like Mississippi, Alabama, and Georgia, singing look how far we've come; only to be taken right back from where we've came. We might as well still be shackled and enslaved like the animals they say we are. The way they treat us, it's as if we're still stuck back in time when they had to march in Selma for the right to vote. Back in time, when they beat the shit out of Nat Turner, hung him high, cut him wide, and took his flesh and some of his organs doing the unthinkable just to keep us niggers in line. They think we've forgotten, but no, we remember everything. It hasn't been hard to forget because they remind us of each chance they get, which is basically every day. Most of them, truth be told, are still looking down on us in disgust, considering us just a bunch of monkeys and lazy untamed niggers. This generation still deals with a lot of racist, ignorant shit too. Donald Trump isn't the only bigot. Not much has changed. They fuck up, do dirty shit, and we still take the blame. We come up with inventions and cures, but they steal the work and claim the fame. They still look down on us, humiliate us, rape, imprison, brainwash, divide, and enslave us all the same. The only difference in the pain we now suffer and the pain our ancestors endured back then is they aren't hanging us from trees anymore. Instead of dragging us down rocky, muddy roads cutting us up and drowning our bodies in the Mississippi River or burning our bodies and crosses, they're shooting our children down over bags of skittles for allegedly acting suspicious. For an iced tea or a purchased pack of cigarettes. We're being slaughtered just because of the color of our skin. Murdered or falsely accused because of who we know or the way we walk, the way we talk, and how we dress. They're taking lives over anything for real. Shaking my head, this cold world is truly a fucking mess. Our kids are being laid out dead in the streets for the world to see like some stray cats and dogs. No child is safe anymore unless you're white, but when it comes down to ours, its fuck them all. They commit hideous crimes and then have the nerve to label us gangsters and criminals when we decide to react.

Like they did when the people protested with Mr. Martin for Trayvon or out in Ferguson when they killed Big Mike. I personally don't see anything wrong with that. Our lives are being jeopardized, so why not fight back? They want to make us look like the aggressors, but we're just responding to the harsh punishments from our oppressors. We're just doing what's necessary, and once again, they've put us under severe attack. They claim all lives matter, but the only ones that count in America are white. They don't give a damn about you if your skin is brown, and you can believe that. They're still trying to serve us nigger pies and tell lies. They don't care about us. I'm telling you. If they did, why is it that the only people really dying from police brutality is black? The racist critics and news media don't agree. That's only because they've long ago stereotyped people the same skin color as me. In their eyes, we never have and never will be shit. They haven't been very discreet when it comes to letting us know that they believe we're all lazy banana-eating monkeys or ignorant cave people. They even used the same words and more to describe our president and the first lady who is black. They're fucking ignorant and don't know what to say. Many of them think they're still better and superior over us just because we're people of color. Most whites, especially the southern ones, have always viewed my sisters and brothers to be unfit. The hate they have for us is real.

Don't believe me? Google what they did to Michael Byrd, Jimmie Lee Jackson, the four little girls killed in the bombing in Montgomery at the church. Read about what they did to Martin Luther King, Trayvon Martin, Michael Brown, Medgar Evers, Sandra Bland, James Earl Chaney, George Winston Lee, and the young boy Emmett Louis Till. Those are only a handful of names that I choose to use, but they're many others that have fallen victim to the abuse. Just yesterday, several police officers dragged Tyrone West out the car by his hair peppered sprayed him, then proceeded to Taser and beat him to death. I've seen so many black bodies young and old lynched, cut up, burned up, or shot up in the street, trees, ditches, roads, highways, alleys, schools, and home broadcasted all over the news. Either that or women and kids being raped, kidnapped, sold as property victims of modern-day slavery, and taken advantage of by the law, a self-proclaimed master, or some other common bastard. They're fearless. Cops shed our blood with ease, acting as if we're their living sacrifice or just simply hate us, and they have nothing to lose. They are killing us off daily. Most times, for no reason. The shit they do is not to be excused. They say we're crazy, but it's them who are out here doing the most. We're out here killing each other; yes, this is also very much true. That nonsense disgusts me, too, don't get it misconstrued or confused. However, we could shoot a different person every day in our hood, and the murder rate at the hands of those who are supposed to serve and protect will never come close. I remember back in the early '90s when the cops beat the shit out of the legendary rapper Tupac Shakur. They damn near killed him; he was lucky to make it to the hospital. Petty cowards did all that to him just for jaywalking, don't let me forget to mention. Predators ended up offering a settlement for a petty amount of money. It's crazy how they've been screwing us over for years. He called their crooked behinds out back then, but of course, they tried to flip the script on him. That's how they operate, never taking responsibility, always placing the blame, or pretending they don't know what happened. How they treat other people of color and us is wrong. Now I know for sure how Moses and his people felt being enslaved to evildoers for so long. We, too, feel the same pain that once caused their tears. Those bastards believe they're the rulers of this entire world, not just us, but I don't recall the Lord ever granting them permission or that position. I find myself asking God what's really good? Do you not see all the foul play that's been taking place worldwide, not just in the ghetto, not just in the gutter, not just in my neighborhood? The world is seriously in shambles. We're facing hard times and current situations that only he can handle. We need him to help us all. Daily we're faced with some sort of trauma. Whether it may be another shooting or people rioting, it's all sorts of drama that involves a bunch of bullshit and possibly somebody's child or mama. I don't know what happened to the change we were supposed to see when we voted for President Obama. I'm still waiting for the day a miracle will happen where there will be no more sickness, hunger, senseless acts of violence, children left behind, racial profiling, unemployment, crowded food, welfare lines, and better opportunities for our youth. The end to the ongoing war and protection for our troops. Almost 8000 American soldiers have died over the years. We all need to stop making shit harder on ourselves and come back together as one. I thought people would pick up the books inspired by one of our own becoming a powerful elected official and put down the gun. I was really hoping for that change, but unfortunately, those days never did come.

With him, in the chair, the Republicans and many others just made shit harder for him and us. He did what they allowed him to. He is the president, but they still hold control over what he can and cannot do. We didn't hit the jackpot like most thought we would be having a black man running the country that came from the hood. He has made minor differences, and some major impacts like making sure some of our rights that had exceeded the statute limitations were still intact. Many don't know that, but I do. It's of high importance, and I'm very grateful for that. If we had let the prejudice white man make the decision, those rights would have been taken back. I give him credit for also catching Osama Bin laden though Isis came right after stronger than ever. I appreciate all the good he and Michelle brought back to all the forgotten neighborhoods. Obama sadly will be leaving the White House very soon. I pray that God will be with us this coming November because if Trump wins, it might fuck around and be another bloody massacre like it was in Chicago July and September. Barack is no saint, but Donald the racist fuck is the devil. He is arrogant, ignorant, and bound to screw us all up on a whole different level. I hope he doesn't win. Many people gave Obama a hard time, especially during his second term. The judgmental jack asses in the media, not just in DC alongside him, criticized him terribly. They act like Bush or any other President before ran the country any better. It really pissed them off, even more, when he joined in on the movement and said black lives matter. Or when he made a speech and said, "If he had a son, his son would look just like Trayvon Martin," it made them hot only cause his sarcastic statement apparently had hit a soft spot. The hate folks have for him is real. Personally, I feel he did what he could. Is there a strong possibility that he could've done more? Yes, but we might as well charge it to the game they had his playbook written out for him in advance the day he first came. I just wish the issues with the police force would be corrected, among other things.

However, this is a President that will go down in history as doing the unthinkable. Who would've ever thought a black man would be sitting in that presidential seat? Didn't make much difference in the streets but still a President that we the people, no matter the color of your skin, will always remember. It will never be another man or couple to grace that White House again the way they did. I'm honored to have been able to witness what my grandparents and ancestors died hoping to see. I say he held his head up high when he has to step down from the throne and be proud. Ronald Reagan, Oliver North, and George Bush Sr. flooded our communities with drugs and guns, creating massive deaths, addictions, arrests, and overdose. This world has been a mess way before he sat in that chair and will still be long after him. If shit doesn't change soon, this country is seriously doomed. The system must do better, and so do we. Change is needed immediately if we want shit to get better. We can't just keep talking about what we need; we have to put in the work, the time, and most importantly put our words into action. We must set the hatred and anger aside, and all play our parts. The cops are not playing fair. They're beyond dirty, but we're fucking up bad too. I'm proud to be black, but I'm not proud of that. I'm very ashamed. I am ashamed of my own actions and thoughts at times but also the actions of others that often make us look bad as a whole. Allowing the drugs and guns that the government ships into our streets through cartels or whoever else they use have become more important than our last breath or the lives of each other. Money, jewelry, clothes, fast cars, technology, violence, gangs, drugs, attention, snaps, likes, and sex have become our ideals. Many of us, including the cops, have allowed these things to become our personal savior. Most call on God only when they're in trouble, stressing, broken, hurt, or need a favor. We need to be calling on him more, however. Somebody has got to step in and put an end to all the brutality and crazy mess. We need him to bring about change to our communities, our churches, and our babies. Education and guidance for our youth. Strength, healing, and medication for the elderly ones. Bibles, books, and balls back in the hands of the troubled ones instead of the normal a bunch of bullets, bottles, blunts, and bodies.

I'm tired of hearing about deaths and mollies; that's why I'm personally taking the time to pray even harder that God can eventually place a change in all of our wicked hearts, putting our devilish ways to rest. I pray for justice. I pray for peace. I honestly believe it would be for the best. I pray for mercy. None of us are truly living as right as we should. I pray for grace. I pray love can eventually replace all the sadness, all the turmoil, and all the hate. I pray we can learn to live in harmony and get along. The way we all treat each other's race from time to time, whether deliberately or not, is wrong. I pray people don't keep believing the hype "TWO WRONGS DON'T MAKE SHIT RIGHT"! An eye for an eye just ends up making everybody blind. We have to put down the weapons and use our mind to fight. We have to start raising more leaders instead of creating a bunch of followers. We need prison reform to be addressed. We need them to understand we're settling for equality and justice only and nothing less. Fuck, keep seeing our loved ones on a t-shirt, and putting murals up everywhere each time another one is placed in the dirt. I need the officers to value our kids' lives more even if they don't know how much they're worth. They can't keep shooting them down like a gang member that walked or rode through the wrong turf. Nor can they keep breaking apart families. It's pure insanity and will eventually destroy the reproduction system making us smaller in numbers. We're tired of suffering from no answers, apology, or justice when those we loved were killed for the entire world to see for nothing. Though most of us were born ford tough doesn't mean colored and Hispanics should be dragged through the mud or treated unjustly. The cops act like we're still the property of the rich white man, and they've got absolutely no love or consideration for us. Forget that the devil is a lie; we aren't items or tools that should be sold or used, nor are we state property. Many of us are still being sold out or purchased for the almighty green dollar. They're shipped state to state, country to country, continent to continent. The public wouldn't believe all the money the government, tricks, and traffickers have spent. They don't see much when they look at us, but when we take a look in the mirror, we have to start seeing more. We have to let our babies know they are important; they are loved, and worth fighting for. We have to let the officers know as of now we will continue to stand our ground. For years we've asked for them to come around; they didn't take us seriously then, but I bet they will now.

We can't continue to carry on like this. I can't stress that enough. I pray we can stand the test of time and remain strong like the strength of a mighty black fist. United and together we aren't easily broken; We're actually much stronger and very outspoken. I pray that our battle for justice will not have to continue too much longer. Lord knows I pray all this suffering hasn't been in vain. We're hurting, losing our relatives or friends; we're yelling out for help wondering when will all the destruction and racial profiling end. We're doing all that we can for ourselves self, but it hasn't really been enough. We're tired of not being taken its seriously as if we're playing poker, and they're trying to call our bluff. We've been treated unjustly for far too many years. I think it's about time we stop being the ones to have to shed a bunch of tears. Crying rivers or should I say sea's going through so much stuff that probably even God himself can't believe. Our hearts are heavy, some of our minds or gone.

Depression is taking a toll; we were stressing over all the things that went wrong. We couldn't just remain silent, and we refused to accept the normal and step off bowing down to the corrupt law. Its time and time are of the essence. We had to step up and stand up now. No more kneeling just doing that is an issue look at how they tried to take away Kapernick crown. I'm glad he made the decision because we're tired of being killed or imprisoned for nothing. We no longer desire to live in fear. Being ignored is no longer an option our voices they now have to hear. Things have got to change. We want and need change. Even if we have to be what changes...

Chapter Two

"Unheard Voices"
We're No Longer Quiet; We're Starting A Riot...

Baltimore City is going fucking crazy. Everybody on one right now from the youth, young adults, and thee old all the way down to the fearless and the bold. Today Mayor Stephanie considered us unstable creatures, wild animals, losers, gangsters, and thugs, but most of the ones that were out there raising hell earlier were our children who obviously could use a few ass whippings along with some love, guidance, care, and hugs. The adults that were out there with them are embarrassing us and acting a fool. They need their ass kicked too. Instead of setting better examples, they're showing out with hoppers nine times out of ten and are probably the ones who were leading the crew. Now is the time to be the parents of our children. They need more than a homie, someone to take selfies with, or a childish acting friend. A lot of us, not just the kids, have issues that need to be addressed. It's real out here on this battlefield. A battlefield, a war zone, dangerous grounds that we're made to call home. Lady Baltimore is hurting; she's been enduring war wounds long before 2016. Her people have been crying for help long before this riot. Pain has been afflicted upon us since way back in the days, so most of the citizens grow up here thinking that maybe crime does pay. Growing up on Gilmore in Bruce courts or any other projects, we have no choice but to go hard. Going hard for many is the only way. Individuals living on the outside have no clue what's it like to live here. They could never handle or imagine the level of suffering this entire city has been through. Yet they judge us from the comforts of their homes or offices on the outside with their nose turned up with many opinions of us as they look in. I heard a spectator say just a few minutes ago on Fox News that the infamous MURDALAND is just reaping all the death we've sown. I beg to differ. Everyone who resides here whether they were born and raised or not are all-out, killing one another or living in sin. Not intentionally anyway. That is for some. Folks like myself actually try to live honestly, make a difference in the community, and try our best to obey God's commandments. We try to live right even in the midst of seeing all the dope and pills being sold or used and the bullets that fly by our head's day and night. It's a jungle out there. Most of us are merely just trying to stay alive. Growing up in impoverished neighborhoods ran by crooked politicians like Shelia Dixon makes it hard for us all to survive. They call us savages, but we're just doing what we have to do.

The only difference between the people they've labeled as thugs throwing bricks or other shit and me is that we take positive legal measurements to ensure justice is served. Protesting peacefully and marching serves a purpose too and has the ability to move mountains for the greater cause. Us nonviolently trying to restore order and be about change, however, is never televised. The media only care to show all the bad stuff that's happening. We all feel the same; we just sometimes resort to other options or resolutions that they may not choose. No one is immune to the trials and tribulations of life. We're all struggling, and all weighed down with a lot of pain. This isn't new shit we just don't react the same. The prime example why I'm angry at the pigs called police dressed in their badges and all blue. I want them held accountable as well; my reaction is just different. How we approach things at times can make a huge difference rather than hollering acting a fool, as they say, causing a scene making all the negative things they already think and say come to be. There's a lot of power that lies in the tongue; although the reaper is near the cops have instilled fear, we can't be moved defeated or distracted by death; we must still speak life into what they want to be a deadly situation. We must resort to other options because they've long ago planned for us to fail; that's why they've subtracted more schools out of the equation and added more jails. They want to keep us in solitude or confinement where misery and depression often lurk around or dwell. History has foretold how they've controlled us and had the upper hand; it's time to write a new story where we rise up.

Fuck so-called lack of evidence, a mistrial, suspension, a paid leave of absence. They are being acquitted of charges, walking away scot-free, going home to live happy lives with their very well and alive family. Taunting us more, flaunting their victory in our faces, but screw all that justice needs to prevail. Had that been one of our black asses doing all the shootings, attempted or committed murder, caught carrying any form of weapons including a gun, we'd be down the bookings swiftly placed in a cell with no bail. I want us to be able to get even too; however, instead of looting petty materialistic possessions like clothes, shoes, and alcohol, I would've been trying to find the right private attorney to represent us and sue. Making sure by the time I was done crucifying their asses in court nailing them to the wall where they belong, the city could feel like Freddie Gray received the justice that we feel is due. Yes, I know no amount of money could ever replace that young man's life, but it could damn sure could bring a little bit of relief to his family's grief and strife. Besides, they have the money they bought 690 suits of Damascus Gear hard- shell body armor for $275,052 with the addition of hundreds more on shoulder shin thigh and forearm guards.

The city of Baltimore spent 2.5 million to be exact all together on riot gear, including $84,480 for next day delivery as protest escalated throughout the city over Freddie's death. Yet so many are homeless, hungry, and hopeless. It's beyond crazy how they can fund the war but can't pay for proper education shelter or food for the less fortunate and the poor. They planned for the people to erupt in advance just like he never really stood a chance. They set out that day to kill someone and why not their normal prey. It's a damn shame what they did to that innocent man. I just don't understand, nor have I seen such a strong outcry or uproar since they left King and many other colored leaking in LA and other states after he was unlawfully beaten and MLK was assassinated.

These cops are dirty as shit, so is the government. Mr. Gray was another black man that was targeted, profiled, and eventually chased down just like Trayvon was. He was unlawfully arrested, attacked, and assaulted. The accused officers claim he had possession of an illegal switchblade that not one witness can account for seeing nor did any of the cameras that recorded his murder. Neither of Freddie's two friends can account for him carrying a concealed weapon with the intent to do bodily harm, nor did they ever recall seeing a knife of any kind. Seeds of hatred weren't the only things planted that day. Their characters were questioned, also demeaned. Their homes were raided on several different occasions for no other reason than to harass or instill more fear. Their rights were violated, their intelligence insulted, and their words fell upon death ears. They were made to give statements about what had occurred. The cops even tried to force them to lie and snitch on some of their other known associates or peers. Their doors have also been kicked in for no reason. Daily they've been stopped and frisked just because. There was even a rumor surfacing that one of his alleged friends was taken to a hidden location then allegedly assed fucked, raped rather, to teach him a lesson for going against them and for showing their deceased partner some love. He told his mother and another strong resource that even a female officer joined in ramming her baton in his behind that she had lubricated and covered with a glove. Humiliation at its best not just degrading. When they finished allegedly, they all laughed then got high off of his drugs. They aren't shit, and that's how they treated Freddie too. The police handled him like some sort of ragdoll and have been telling mad lies or covering up their wrongdoings since then. The stories have changed numerous times, but a lot of stuff just doesn't add up, and the videos tell a completely different story. I find it hilarious that they're now trying to play the victim; they must be suffering from some type of mental disability too. None of them has admitted to what they did, and they probably never will. Not even one has taken the time out to apologize or make things right, then wonder why we think they enjoy taking another life. Whether he had a knife or was running for his life or not, they were wrong, and that man was done dirty no matter how they try to sugarcoat it.

They took making a simple stop and search or arrest to the extreme and did it with the help of their team. I'm talking about his leg being broken, him basically tortured, injuries to his spinal cord, and then left suffering in the back of a hot patty wagon pleading for his life. The bastards threw him in headfirst unsecured, resulting in a coma, which eventually led to his unfortunate death. I can't stop watching the video of him begging for mercy. Each time I feel like he knew he only had minutes left. The officers, several who are of color, did everything but their job that day. Now it seems the chief, the district attorney office, none of them involved fucking care, nor do they have any remorse or sympathy for the victim. They don't agree one of them should have to do jail time or pay; they see absolutely nothing wrong. I wonder, does God hear us crying since they don't? I wonder if God will help us save us show some concern since they won't? The city really all the black communities around the world are in a lot of agonizing pain. The numerous amounts of deaths have put on a serious strain, not just detrimental stress to our already overwhelmed brains.

We're all hurting for and with him. I feel the rage of the city. I just choose another way of making them feel my wrath. What they did was wrong; they had no empathy at all. Heartless scum bags even made stop after stop harassing other people in the neighborhood neglecting Freddie and his needs. They gave no medical treatment or calls for paramedics, although he continued to ask for help; this is what the media consider a good cop. Bullshit! Can you believe they just threw him in the back of that patty wagon like a piece of yesterday's trash? Hurting, helpless, begging for oxygen to breathe, but he was denied. Due to all those well-known factors, he slowly but surely died from all his injuries. Many rules were broken by so-called trained officers that day, and due to their vicious attack, Freddie is no longer. His family is not only furious they're devastated, so is the rest of the city, especially his two friends that were with him and other residents around Gilmore Homes in thee Sandtown – Winchester neighborhood. The city is heartbroken, not just upset. We find it hard to believe they basically killed him on camera for no reason, and the police chief doesn't want to take those dirty ass cops down. We colored folk as a whole have been going through it again for some years now, but not once did many imagine it would hit so close or also affect our homes directly. Job descriptions and duties were neglected, his request was rejected, but all the bullshit was expected.

It isn't the first time they've been put under pressure or the scope, nor is it the last time they will give false statements or hope. His death went viral quickly, but they still refused to disclose any type of real information to the public and are allowing the police to continue harassing other residents in that community, especially Freddie's two homeboys that were with him when the tragedy occurred. Instead of trying to the right their wrongs and restore some sort of order so that we may all be able to get along, they've just continued to be on their best bullshit. They've been bashing Mosby and even considering bringing charges against her. They're in their feelings because thanks to the outcry of the people and her, they may end up doing some time. Oh well, they all deserve it, although there are many who may not agree. My personal opinion is fuck twelve.

They've deliberately gone out their way to make our lives a living hell. If they only knew if only, they cared how they're making, we the people feel. The officers claim what the media and streets say isn't true, but we all know their trigger-happy behinds are being dishonest. Cameras don't lie. The proof is in the pudding. Nobody told them to take deadly precautions that real trained officers know they shouldn't. I don't care what they or the mayor says what they did was wrong. It's going to take a miracle and a lot of time for his family, the rest of us here in the city, and around the world to let this incident die down and eventually move on. Just acting like our lives don't matter is hard to do. We can't just turn the blind eye or the other cheek anymore; they've gotten way too carried away with this type of nonsense.

Furthermore, they've been doing dirt for way too long and getting away with it. I support the black lives matter movement one hundred percent. The cops are trying to destroy us all, but we are not going to have that shit. The year nearly comes to an end, and over 500 people have been shot and killed worldwide by police officers alone sad truth. Most of the cops involved in the incidents have never been charged, arrested, or convicted, that is ridiculous. We're sick of being hurt and harassed. We're tired of being the victims of a racist, crooked, and money-hungry judicial system. A system that I feel was never really designed to protect or serve us coloreds in the first place regardless of the wolf tickets they try to sell us. I believe it was really created to divide us. It was created to conquer and destroy us. They made it to keep us down locked in the Bing or in the box, barely surviving in the projects that they flooded with heroin and ready rock. They've tried to place limitations on our lives and everything we busted our asses working hard for, placing countless limitations on things we earned or the assets we have as if many of us come from a lot. Slavery really isn't over; they just try dressing it up. We've never been treated equally, and it's only because of our race. The greedy white man has never given a fuck about nothing but black or foreign pussy, power, and an easy, quick buck. We aren't free in this land, nor is anything in it, not even the air we breathe in.

Their actions constantly remind us and show us that they still don't consider us to be equals. They didn't include us African Americans when they said, "WE THE PEOPLE ". I don't even feel like we're American, nor am I still proud to be one. So once again, I say I do understand the anger and frustration of my people and the people of the city, but at the same time, I know rioting or looting isn't the way. Acting out in such a negative manner with all the cameras rolling just gives them more ammunition and excuses to keep messing with us. Violence only begets more violence. Killing them in revenge will not make us safe or guarantee us a brighter day. In my opinion, it's only going to engulf an already hot flaming fire, making things much harder on us and causing more lives to be lost, making an already fucked up situation much worst.

As I continue to watch the news and all the troops, I grow overwhelmed with anxiety and fear. I'm afraid and not ashamed to admit it. Not of them in particular but of another one of us being placed in a black hearse. Shit real, and we are truly living on a battlefield. I'm glad we were born war-ready. They brought the tanks out on us today; it looked like a scene from Vietnam. Hell, for a minute there, I thought the heartless fucks might even drop a bomb. You never know what these cowards will do next. I haven't seen any stuff like this or read about it since all the riots back in the day that occurred in New York, Baltimore, and Los Angeles in the '60s. We're living in a fucking war zone. It's not safe in the streets; it doesn't matter if you drive, catch the bus, or walk. We've become the hunted ones. There's no telling what's going to happen when the cameras leave, and all the lights and fires are put out. I hate even to predict it, but I can see a few more bullets-riddled bodies lingering in the streets for the cleanup man to collect. I can just about imagine how many of the so-called thugs they will eventually lay down when they think the world has stopped looking and no more spectators are around. I'm more than certain it will be countless bodies somewhere stinking after being executed like a piece of a worthless piece of trash left to rot in the middle of the road or a park. I can see innocent children or elderly men and women getting secretly hurt, caught up in this madness, just as soon as they think the world is no longer watching, and it's dark. I can see pistols being fully loaded up on both sides, equipped with massive artillery eagerly awaiting the precious moment to murder their mark. If people shared the same thoughts as me or knew what I know, they would go inside their homes and just respect the curfew that's been set for us all if they're smart. The cops aren't playing fair neither is the national guards or the families like myself that still have to reside here or be caught out there. I pray for our communities and for our churches when all the smoke, looters, onlookers, law enforcement, and media clear because when the sun rises in the morning, guess what we all still have to live here. For many of us residing here in the city, there are no other options; some have no idea what the rest of the outside world look likes because they've never even had the opportunity to visit another state or left the only place they've always known. What you see is what you get because so many are stuck inside of a box afraid to step out on faith. Many are too concerned about what folk going to say as if they still aren't going to talk reckless about them anyway.

Too many addicted to smoking, using, manufacturing, or distributing drugs that they've forgotten they're worth more. Sadly, they've unfortunately started to believe everything the opposition said although we know deep inside, we're not. There are a million reasons why some have never left and might not ever see the outside of these city walls times being hard, and everybody thinking they're above the law are just a few obstacles that have enabled or prohibited individuals from doing their best or what they really wanted too. In desperate times also out of anger and frustration, we stoop to measurements that we may not have thought to do before. Some of us stoop extremely low endangering ourselves and also others. It's that exact type of bullshit and negative way of thinking we have to let go of if we really want change. All that food, medication, and other essentials to live a healthy life that's now become a complete waste for the gutters is just going to make it harder for many to be able to put a roof over their heads and food on their plates. Burning CVS and those other stores were just pure stupidity. We're our own enemies as well! Often times we just don't realize that because we're too caught up in our feelings, too caught up in the past, too eager to make a dollar fast, too busy complaining or placing blame on others for the life that we feel we have to live in hell. We're quick to cry victim, but we inflict pain upon ourselves too. Some are in denial when it comes to accepting our own truths and even worst our ignorant behavior, showing and sending out the wrong example and a bunch of mixed messages to our future: the youth. We must start doing better by ourselves first before we can ask that of anyone else.

We have to care more about ourselves and our communities. We have to be the help we're often asking for. We all have to do better; it's simply no other way to put it. Those stores, malls, pharmacies, and bus routes, among other things destroyed, are a major necessity for us all in one way or another. When their asses wake up tomorrow in need, they will then realize looting and committing arson hurt us only. Not only that, the way we choose to respond enables the officers to come with more force, being even more violent, not just aggressive, hostile, and ignorant with our children, our pastors, our siblings, our friends, our fathers, and mothers. Though we're throwing all the bullshit back at them that they've expected us to live in and with forever, we could've maybe tried to humble ourselves and handled this situation a little better. This city really needs help. Lady Baltimore needs Jesus right now, like no place other.

I wonder how much longer God can continue just to sit and watch us suffer. Freddie Gray wrongful death has become a trending topic along with many other murders, and I don't foresee any of it coming to an end. You see how even on the day that the young man is being laid to rest, people are still very upset, raging with fire out in the streets and town hall still going all the way in. They sent Marilyn Mosby out, which is the States Attorney, to sell us wolf tickets to calm us down. Shorty tried to ensure us justice will be served, but we have to chill out and first let them do their job. I doubt that's seriously happening if anything her and those officers mess around and be the next one's dead or robbed. I believe they only decided to prosecute the accused officers due to trying to calm the storm they caused here in the city. They're really not concerned about us being treated unfairly; they just don't want us to burn this bitch down completely. Nor do they want all these angry "black "people in the back yards or front lawns. As we saw today, half the city is already blazing, so I think they're starting to get an idea of what we're capable of doing when were under severe pressure and pissed off extremely. We've been pushed way past our limits. How much more do these oppressors really expect people to take? I know patience is a virtue, but the clock is running out. We're tired of being unheard and overlooked. We're tired of being mistreated, humiliated, murdered, harassed, beat up, kidnapped, sold as property, and watching our loved ones be manhandled or imprisoned for nothing.

We're fucking tired of being a victim of a huge police or political scandal. That's why Tom Cat's mother still sniffing dope sitting home, nodding out when she supposed to be watching her girl Olivia Pope. While many are progressing forward despite the many obstacles at hand, others have given up fighting back physically or just lost all hope. I ask God daily how much longer must we suffer? Have thou not already endured enough? We're tired of watching our family members being done wrong by a racist, biased, heartless prick wearing a metal badge that makes him think he is superior over Latinos, Blacks, Foreigners, and other minorities. Wearing that badge makes them feel like they have a certain amount of power and control over us. Their egos are big because their small minds inside large heads have been blown up. We've been ignored and taken advantage of not just overlooked. We've also been made to accept them being unlawful, dishonest, thieves, who're prejudice with no conscious and are very corrupt. It's like they're wearing an invincible cape with a big "S" on their chest. They believe their titles or stature will stop them from getting a hole in their vest. Fuck boys, followers, want to be gangsters, but cowards for real. I can't say anything less my mouth is reckless just like them right now because we've been put under constant scrutiny and duress. They bribe, extort, threaten, and payoff informants to come to court; they do everything they shouldn't be doing but lack in the department of protecting and giving the prosecuting team or relatives any form of support. They never take responsibility for their actions; instead, they move like the Italian mafia pretending to be so tough but can't fight a lick. Must likely soft guys that got bitched during high school, and now the badge has blown his or her head up, and now they can't handle it. Power, too, just like drugs is highly addictive.

They refuse to abide by the law or any type of rules. These cops are pulling pistols on unarmed folk more than a carpenter uses his tools. They're the real thugs, real live gangsters, the real criminals, and the real heartless fools. How they treat us is messed up, it's unfair. They let their little positions and uniforms go to their fucking head, I swear. Funny right? Now they're the same ones out here on Penn and North Ave playing the victims as if they haven't been the ones filling our family members and friends up with lead. They love playing dumb after they've done dirt and left someone's loved one numb. It seems each, and every one of them suffered from amnesia when interrogated lying about a gun.

Prime example, an officer entered the home of someone else illegally, killing the tenant instantly just for being in the residence he paid bills in. The female officer claims the victim had broken into her house, but it was actually vice versa.

Meanwhile, across the parking lot, another tenant was accused of not belonging and acting suspiciously by just being black caught off guard in his own apartment. Crazy also racist white female cop claim to mistake his place for her own she thought there had been a burglar awaiting her arrival back home. Shorty says she's done no wrong her life had been threatened with his presence alone, but okay, the man was where he laid his head. What more do I need to say? Her ass is guilty of being racist, intoxicated, and a murderer, but first, that has to be proven in a court of law. However, the majority of the time, when charges are actually brought up in most cases, they have still been found not guilty or acquitted. "They're innocent," says the judge "They couldn't have done it." "These men and women are honest, hardworking officers," they say, but we beg to differ.

They're just as bad if not worse than Adolf Hitler. It's not cool, and this brutality has got to stop. I'm tired of seeing the yellow tape and red bloodstains. Women out in the streets half naked, going hysterical, distraught each time they look down on the ground, shocked at all the scattered fragments and pieces of what was once their loved one's brains or heart. It's no fun having to identify your loved ones remains. Situations like that leave our lives forever changed. Many are still traumatized suffering from post-traumatic stress disorder or strung out on pills getting high daily just to cope. There are no way things can stay the same.

Personally, I don't see why the hell they expect us to. Look at all the stuff we're constantly being put through. It's not a good feeling hearing or seeing the aftermath of those you know or care about that have been slain. I'm tired of seeing many people living here in the city walking around carrying all this hurt. I pray the Lord can stop us all from putting one another in the dirt. I say all of us I don't just blame the white man or cops for all the tragic situations we face in this so-called free land; We've also demonstrated actions of an ignorant person that just doesn't give a damn. Though they're the leading cause of most causes of death outside of gang shootings, I blame us too for killing each other off. It hasn't only been the crackers behind the reasons for us having to wear so many rests in peace t-shirts. Our hands are also bloody too many have just chosen to act oblivious to the fact. We have to reach one then teach one.

Constantly stressing the importance of picking up the balls, microphones, books, and a pen putting down the knives, gun, and other things that could land us dead in the trap or caged like animals in pen. If we stand together as the mighty powerful fist that we once were, moving with an unbreakable force, using our minds as weapons, we can still beat them or overcome. Showing our natural black asses isn't the way to conduct ourselves. Little stupid shit like that just gives them a reason, another excuse for all the trifling stuff that they've got a tendency to do. God, your people, are going through it. I probably say that a hundred times a day only because it's true the city does need you. I wonder, does he hear me? Does he hear us calling? We're stuck between a rock and a very hard place. Handling the situation like some of us did acting like pure fools just make us look dumb. In the same sentence, I sometimes do; however, find violence may be necessary. I don't want us to continue to be our own ruin, but real talk with some people or certain situations there's no other way. It's as if we're damned if we do and damned if we don't know when it comes to running this race.

They claim we're a threat, but we're the ones who are really going through it. Many have snapped and lost all hope. I, on the other hand, I'm praying Jesus can be a fence, and eventually, all that we've had to endure, we will eventually grow through. This city, along with many others worldwide, needs God's help seriously! I wonder, does he at least hear us crying? The media, the Mayor, the spectators, the law enforcement, the troops, or the Governor obviously damn sure don't. We're done asking them for the help and the justice we deserve because, as you can see, we already know they won't. Those motherfuckers don't care about us; they don't live in the real world that we're in, nor do they have to worry about being subjected or accustomed to the harsh realities that we have had too. They don't have any of the worries we have while they sit comfortably in the suburbs stress-free every year.

Those inconsiderate degenerates really don't care I'm telling you. Look how long it took the Mayor even to show her face. It took way to long for our supposed to be a leader to respond. When she did, it sounded as though she had also lost her mind. I'm no way proud of how some of us chose to react to the injustice we've been made to grow accustomed to for so long, but how she tried to downplay her own city and the people of our communities was dead ass wrong. She tried correcting it but was too late. The cameras recording had already caught it. We all heard her loud and clear. Her harsh words spoke volumes. I don't foresee her arrogant inconsiderate behind being reelected anytime soon. Well, maybe I should just say she won't be getting my vote. How she addressed, the situation was somewhat very offensive to many, not just me. We all felt in some form or fashion that the way she spoke of us and our children was not right. Last time I checked, she resided in Baltimore too. The people were venting, lashing out, crying, and pleading for help for understanding, but Ms. Stephanie Rawlings Blake was out of sight. She probably was busy making sure her face was beat to the gods or trying to get her whack speech together before she took her place at the podium fronting for the cameras on the mic. We, the community, feel like she doesn't really care about us either. It angers me personally others as well to see how she pretends for the cameras as if before Freddie's death, life here in the city was all good. It's distasteful that the mayor and others who held power to fix the situation weren't doing all the things that they know they promised during the campaign. Everything they said turned out to be lies; So many were told I had to knock on wood for them. We the people have been pleading our cases for a very long time, but the news reporters or other people such as Mayor Rawlings never step a foot in our hood. Not until today, that is, when they started a riot or when death came in huge numbers rapidly. Before that, all of them were missing in action, brushing us off or doing all they can to hush us up and keep our always complaining about something behinds quiet. The only time they seem to have something to say or show face is when they're trying to make us look bad just as they did earlier. They enjoy airing all the negative things about our home but disregard and ignore anything that we try to do that is positive just as they did once again today.

They showed all the looting, the chaos, the violence, the

rioting, the so-called injured officers, and everything else that was fucked up about the situation but shed no light or camera time on the peaceful protests, the positive marches, the leaders of the community, and preachers trying to talk the outraged crowd down or the much-needed prayers let me not forget that. They ignored us taking a bow in the middle of the streets for a moment of peace and silence. They also ignored the youth and older ones who set out to make a difference nonviolently and all the gangs praying together, hoping to bring about a ceasefire. I find how they try to expose us very sad. Those of us who chose to remain nonviolent wasn't relevant to the horrific picture of Baltimore that they were trying to paint because we moved in peace, compassion, and silence. We marched for a greater cause, one in which we weren't looking for recognition, extra attention, or applause. We just wanted to see a change come about ASAP that will not take us back down that old route from which we've already had to travel many times.

Baltimore has come a long way, yes, but yet we're already still trying to repair and recover from the riot that destroyed our communities back in the day. There are still many homes boarded up, and other properties still condemned that was destroyed during the riot when MLK was shot to death. It's so much that has yet to be repaired. We really need God to step in and intervene; my words today are not just a dream or something of make-believe. This here is all real talk like the discussions at the Red Table with Mrs. Jada Pinkett Smith. I'm praying for my second home and the city from which she was actually born and the streets our children have to walk. These days you just don't know, nor can you be too sure; It's a war zone out here. None of us are safe here or on foreign soil must certainly if your skin color is anything but white. God, we need you I know none of this has taken you by surprise even though we couldn't foresee any of the troubles that lied ahead of us. We're in a great state of shock, hurt, and disbelief, not just sorrow or grief. Life is hectic around my way, and a lot of innocent lives are taken in between just due to trying to survive each day. We're enduring so much the media and city officials just make sure it doesn't get seen. From the west side to the east from the hustler to the little innocent girls and boys playing in the streets, we're all liable to be the next to get shot in the head with that infrared beam. They want that outside of our home to believe we are the bad guys, but they're the ones doing dirty shit and covering it up with lies. As they speak on behalf of the accused officers, I can see the deceit in their eyes. Trust me; their hands are far from clean. How do you think most of them got to where they are today? It damn sure wasn't from them just chasing the so-called American dream. They're full of it, I swear, it's okay though I know judgment day if nothing else will always be there. They get away with a lot of shit here on earth, but it's a completely different story once they too hit the dirt.

They will eventually have to pay the piper one day, whether that be right now or later. I hope there's no mercy shown either; they deserve no favor. Not trying to come off as an asshole who's heartless just like them, I'm merely just saying. They need to be held accountable because I doubt they will be at the trial. It's so many glitches in the case I can already see this being dragged out for a long while. We all know they're guilty, but they're going to do everything to dispute the charges. I bet you a lot of evidence that supposed to be concealed will find its way in the garbage. They're going to do whatever to try to cover up the truth. That's what they do best, but as long as they continue to operate in the same fashion, this city won't be getting too much rest. Freddie Gray death was no accident or mistake; this is a test that has everybody under duress. I'm praying we can claim victory and be triumphant over all this mess. It's not looking good for the city right now. I'm still wondering what's going to happen when they put all the hoses away and take the roadblocks down. I'm very concerned. The looks the troops have on their faces let me know that they came prepared for a fight. I really don't believe peace and restoring order is why they were called in tonight. Many here in the city are in their homes scared to death watching from afar. They, too, are very much concerned about all that has transpired today. They're also worried about if they live to see it what will happen tomorrow. Truth be told, so am I. The streets are a mess. Cars and buildings are on fire, and the cost to repair everything will probably go through the roof. What wasn't damaged was taken, used, or sold. I hear people got some hot stuff for sale right at this very moment down on Booth street. To some, it may seem like the cool thing to do, but whether they may realize it or not, they're going to require a lot of that shit they just destroyed, and I'm speaking nothing but the truth. So much of that stuff rolling down the street, thrown in gutters, or set on fire could've been put to good use. This looting bullshit is just another example of what I mean when I say we are our own enemies at times. We, too, do stupid shit acting out before we take the time to think about the consequences of our actions fully. We inflict unnecessary pain amongst ourselves and others with no thought in hopes that we won't be exposed or caught. Shouldn't our lives matter just as much even during those trying times as well, or at least I thought? Some robbed the drug stores just to get a free fucking high. They didn't think about those who would really need that supply. Thoughts of how we conducted ourselves this afternoon makes me want to cry. Someone's grandparents won't be able to get their medication cause the pharmacy will now be closed. Somebody will need to catch a bus that normally runs on the route where most of the tragedy took place earlier, and they may very well be canceled or rerouted, taking people off of their daily schedule or routine. Someone's child may not make it to school tomorrow because the parent is too afraid to send them out. The way all the schools are being shot up too can you really blame them. One bad apple can spoil the entire bunch is one thing I'm trying to get some to understand. I say it out of love not to bring guilt or shame. It's real out here. The dangerous atmosphere has them worried their babies could be shot down and killed as well without a doubt. I don't blame them either. Lives are being taken away from here daily over dumb shit like poor judgment, hatred, money, drugs, positions, titles, or clout. Making shit harder for ourselves wasn't what the protest was supposed to be about. It was supposed to be the time we stood together again for a greater cause instead of standing against one another for the all mighty green dollar, greed, pussy, envy, or jealousy. It was time to put all of our issues and frustrations into words. It was the time for us to stand together as a mighty black fist and be triumphant over the oppressor who wishes to continue to act like people of color don't matter or deserve the right to be heard. It was the time to let them know we're no longer accepting their asses to kiss. It was time for the babies to be able to speak because law enforcement and politicians ignore the poor, immigrants, and the people whom they perceive to be weak. It was time to let them know we no longer want to settle for their small handouts such as welfare, we demand more sources of employment, education, and pay that's fair. It was the time to let them know our family members' bodies will not keep entering the coroner's office or making the front headline of the paper or the next breaking story on the news. It was the time to let them know we aren't property or test dummies for the state that they can just manipulate or misuse. It was time to let them know we're very aware of our rights though they try to paint a picture that we're just a bunch of fools. It was time to let them know we aren't our ancestors; we will not just bow down we fucking refuse. The media airing all the negatives made a lot of people miss the point or the severity of the circumstances at hand.

The real message got overlooked by all the mess. It was time to let them know that we can stand. Stand strongly united together for something instead of murdering each other over nothing. It was the time for us to rise up again, staying focused on the task not being distracted like they wanted by other meaningless things that were occurring at the same time or bound to happen. Grabbing a pistol is easy; it took more courage more strength to use our mind as a weapon but still moving with aggression if need be. We wanted the rest of the world to see just how difficult it is to live with the same skin color as me. It was the time to let them know us black folks have had enough; That we're more than just a pack of wild animals who were thirsty for attention. We chose to cut up instead of just simply speaking our peace without fear of being gunned down faster than they can muster the words shut up. It was time to let them know we will not continue to be moved or tolerate the constant brutality even if it means calling their bluff. The extra bullshit and nonsense took away the real focus at hand. We have to calm down so we can really get justice not just for Freddie but for every innocent woman, child, and man. I want our voices to be heard. I want our pain to be felt. I want justice to be served as well, but we have to play our cards much smarter, no matter the fucked- up hands that so many of us have been dealt with. God willing in due time, I believe we will prevail even if they all don't be charged or thrown into jail.

Chapter Three

"Cold Hearted World"
This Can't Be Life Too Many Are Crooked Or Cruel For Us Nothing Is Going right...

This is a dirty, hateful, cold, and unjust world we live in. As I write today, I find myself sitting in a state of shock and disbelief over the many tragic things that have currently happened. More dead bodies laid out all over the news and cases of women suffering from domestic violence and abuse. Many are being brutally stabbed or held against their will if not being beaten, enslaved, treated as pets, and pissed on by perverts like Jeffrey Epstein or R. Kelly. Robert, who's also obsessed with weak grown woman and children, has been accused of being a sex cult leader who's brainwashing teenage naïve young girls like the one he's alleged to be holding hostage from here. Bizarre accusations have been made, although he denies those allegations. I personally believe those women are all telling the truth regardless if some may have been a little thirsty. They didn't deserve that no woman or child does, but here in America and other countries, many are demeaned by the entire organization or team. Children and adults are being manipulated and taken advantage of by predators who can barely read or write but smuggling in more pussy than the narco's in the tunnels at night. They're killed, forced to take drugs, battered, and bruised by their violent captors. Some are sold into misery by greedy parents who're also a group of heartless bastards. Billions of dollars are made while millions of men, women, and children are being held captive forced to do free labor and be sex slaves. The number of victims would have you amazed. They say there's a child born every day, but there's also victims of sex trafficking birthed daily as well. Kids are having kids way too early then imprisoned for murder or child neglect because they couldn't handle the pressure of crying baby and decided it was best them or their mate cause harm to the child, possibly snapping their necks. Some of the parents are out there right along with them fucking out of both pant legs like they don't know any better, degrading themselves, dropping out of school, destroying their temples, leaving grandparents with the burden of having more hungry parentless children to raise. Having sex out of wedlock lusting sleeping around like the HIV virus isn't real, along with other sexually transmitted diseases. These old heads, not just the young girls are out here clout or thrill chasing behind a dope boy a dollar and a dream while he chasing behind junkies for sex, fake Gucci belt's, when they really didn't create their attire for people like ourselves. Lean, pills, cheap thrills, likes on Instagram, molly, or weed seem to be all people want or need. The crooked ass politicians still selling us citizens a bunch of high-priced heroin, lies, and oil, among other things. Pussy and children are the top sellers, along with tons of false dreams. Too many folks are selling themselves short for a pack of tracks, expensive cars, houses, a luxurious handbag, the newest Jordan's, drugs, and titles. For money, sex, and the finer things people will do anything. Some are killing each other for less beefing over childish mess or being thirsty for attention, doing whatever for a free high, welfare checks, liquor, or discounts on a new body part of figure. I just don't understand half the shit these young and older people do in the name of love, to have an significant other to claim, to display a status of having a relationship or financial wealth on the internet, for fortune and fame, to fit in with the crowd or to bears someone's position or last name. It's many doing whatever basically just to fit in, trying their hardest to be accepted, loved, not overlooked, or rejected. Going in debit struggling, even more, trying to keep up with the Joneses like so many have done before. As if they will give more fucks about them than they did when spending their last at a store. Going out our way to please folk who could really care less that will still talk about you if you're doing good or bad. They're looking for validation searching for approval idealizing gangs and all the wrong things eagerly awaiting the time to be jumped in. I thought dust was the only stuff that's supposed to settle, but unfortunately, it's a lot of human beings out here accepting whatever as if playing the position of a fool or settling for less is going to gain them credit or a damn gold medal. To heck with followers, likes on a post, or so-called street cred none of that shit matters because you can't take it with you when you gone. It pays off more to do right than to limit yourself, accept having nothing, or being nothing and living wrong. We really need to do better. I'll be glad when they make a challenge to stay in school and out of jail. The negative image many older ones sometimes portray has a major impact and influence on our youth. Many may not want to accept what I just said but I don't care because it's nothing but the truth. Then they wonder why half of our children stay locked up somewhere behind bars and a fence doing an extensive bid. Lack of leadership, guidance, knowledge, love, and understanding mixed with too much technology is destroying these fucking kids. A girl died recently hanging with the wrong people over some petty Facebook beef. She was found dead a day later burned to death after first having been stabbed repeatedly. The assailants boasted and bragged about it on their pages with no shame or remorse for the victim or her loved ones. They were proud of the so-called work they had put in, but that young lady's family isn't so enthused about what happened. Two twin girls assaulted, brutally attacked, stabbed, and eventually drowned their own mother to death. As she fought for her last breath they coldly laughed about the matter as if they had another mother no one knew about left. The girls went to school late the same morning after committing such a heinous crime pretending, they hadn't just lost their mind. They even had the audacity to play the role of someone who was shocked and sadden. The burst with joy inside it had to take a lot of acting to force the fake tears, of course, when they were being questioned by the law. This world is crazy, and many people in it are pure evil, not just shady.

I don't understand why some people just can't seem to want or just do better than this. This type of foolishness doesn't make sense. Guess they prefer to live life wild, selfish, careless, and free. Out for self, not giving a damn about nobody else. Yelling out Y.O.L.O is the motto they live by. They enjoy acting out for the world to see. I don't think they realize their actions are the reasons why the crackers and many others are critical, fearful, and judgmental of us blacks and other minorities. If only they knew what they could become or all the extra shit, we're forced to go through. If only they knew that the statement of only living once isn't really true. My personal opinion is if a person chooses to live right by God or whatever their higher power is and not the world, we will all have the opportunity to rise up again. I believe on the third day, he rose up, and I also believe we have the ability to do the same. The only way I can see us condemned to hell is by not obeying Moses' commandments: not repenting and by trying to refrain from sinning. We could never be perfect; this is very true, but we always have the option of trying to be the best person we can be. We all have the option of trying to do better. I suggest the kids stay focused on the books instead of trying to be lifelong crooks, or instead of picking up guns, pick up a pen or a ball. I know those parents who had to bury a child was devastated when they received that terrifying call. I don't have any children of my own, but I can only imagine how it feels. I find myself hurting for them all. It's so much pain floating around the world, not just the city. Times have changed drastically, and a lot of people have become grimy, devilish, and gritty. It's not just the adolescents who are out of control; some of the adults are showing their ass as well or just being lazy, complaining because they've done nothing but fail.

The outcome of all that inconsistency I'm sure will be everything but pity. I don't trust law enforcement truthfully, not a soul. In this day and time, you really can't. All sorts of crimes are being committed, and it seems like a lot of folks have just gone crazy and snapped. I'm talking about so far gone that God or Jesus himself probably couldn't bring them back. There are psychopaths out here killing their own damn parents, grandparents, and sadly also their own kids. So many children have been drowned, poisoned, mutilated, smothered, or beaten to death. You got people killing innocent folk just for material possessions, family estates, the newest trend, money, or the way a person may choose to live. Guns are taking lives rapidly, and the filthy toxic water in Flint, Michigan, is killing the kids, but they neglected to tell people about the lead or the trifling stuff they did. It took five months for them even to make the hazardous situation publicly known. So many are struggling to live beneath the poverty line, where many have had no other choice but to adapt to a life of crime. Daily, the media gets a full report broadcasting live from the projects about how someone's son has been shot, someone's daughter got kidnapped, a bank robbery, drug deals have gone wrong, or dysfunctional family's that can't seem to get along.

Playgrounds lined off in yellow tape, teenagers yelling rape, countless funerals being planned due to all the gang violence that's gotten out of hand. Corruption within the government is at an all-time high, and Isis is steadily on the rise. More bombings have recently occurred over the weekend 29 people were injured in

Manhattan while five explosive devices were found in Elizabeth, New Jersey, at a train station. Ahmad khan Rahamid is the alleged suspect whom I might add is still alive, he took one to the leg, I believe, but that's about it. None of the city streets are safe. They're deadly, and anybody can get it. I'm not just speaking about terrorists either because there are many others who pose a serious threat, and they too are citizens of the United States. Those streets don't love or care about anybody; it just takes away from you most times. Not just your freedom, but all that you love, including your possessions, can all be gone away within the blink of an eye. Some might not want to believe that because the money and alleged street cred has them blind. They think the streets love you, but they don't really love you back; some just never take heed. If they do, it may have taken them forever to realize that. I'm speaking from personal experience. I've seen so many get swallowed up whole, but that's another story that in due time will be told. I just want to emphasize the consequences of the streets and the game. It's not for everybody, and you'll gain everything in the end but glory or fame. I know for millions it's the way they survive; it's the only option they feel they have to maintain, but I rather see those individuals reach out for other opportunities because I'm tired of my people being incarcerated or are in early graves. It is becoming another statistic or a waste of pure talent and potential washed down the drain. Shit real in the streets.

No one is exempt. However, getting back to the actual topic at hand if it isn't some bullshit like that being the topic of conversation, they might be discussing a robbery, leaked sensitive information, a documentary on O.J Simpson, or crooked politicians and their latest scams. It could be either one of those things or a combination of them all. Aspiring to be the next American gangster, many of our youth and my fellow old heads idealize the gold they love the glory, but they have no real knowledge of who these gangsters are or true understanding of themselves or the other side of their stories. They see the fast money and fame, but they don't see the death and destruction that comes with dealing drugs, no matter if its marijuana or cocaine. No matter who you are, no matter your pedigree, no matter your stature or street credibility, the outcome will always be the same. The player and time are the only thing that

will ever change. I've lost so many friends and family members to early graves or prison cells. I've seen pressure make the toughest, the so-called best of them fold. I've seen good people turn dirty, and their hearts turned wicked and cold. I've seen children abused, raped, or sold. I've seen death, and the effects of drugs take a serious toll. Now it seems the entire world is at odds or out of control. It never fails, each time I turn on the television, I'm hearing about how somebody killed somebody. It's sad there are no more safe zones for us. Not even at a lot of the kid's schools or colleges. What's not already condemned is being shot up or in the midst of being shut down because many are already in the state of Missouri, Chicago, Maryland, and many other places as well in the US.
The workplace, the market, the rec center, or the pool, along with other public places, aren't safe either. I used to think half the shit the media said was a joke, but life quickly made me a believer. That's because it's too many people packing guns, addicted to some type of drugs, walking in the streets with no care in the world just itching to do whatever for a fix or to body a fool. Some bullshit just kicked off yesterday that I didn't think was cool. I'm hearing the Knockers murdered this young dude I know from around the way. To make matters worse than what it already is, six more lives have just been taken right now as we speak today. Three young girls were found in a pond dead due to wrecking their vehicle, eventually drowning, trying to allude the police in a stolen car. All three were of color, not one suspect over the age of sixteen, all troubled with records, and uneducated. To me, that's really pathetic; it's also sad. Their track records with the law were worse than your average lifetime crook. The media labeled the teens troubled and bad. Less than an hour after that aired, a black news reporter was said to have lost his mind flipped out, killing several other employees cause his former coworkers were judgmental towards him for being gay. The man went crazy, but I'm not surprised, this isn't the first time a situation like this has occurred. Jamal, as the world knows him on empire was just attacked beaten and attempted to be lynched allegedly anyway. Others have been victims as well of biased homophobic individuals or just ignorant folk who're full of hatred just because. The world has been in a huge debate over religion, oil, and money, but most of all, arguing over the LGBT

community and equal rights for a while now. Donald Trump and a lot of people have a problem with homosexuality, but not the way this fucked up country is being run. We aren't free to be who we are anymore; many are making us very uncomfortable in our own skin. Love is love and who are we as humans to sit around and judge. People who are considered gay, that way, funny, weird, or unfit have been enduring a lot of brutality, injustice, and strife as well.

Everybody has something to say about those with lifestyles that differ from theirs. I don't see them talking about the pope or the preacher who's fucked all the nuns and children in the church or the police chief that gets high, abuses his wife and kids. If you're a celebrity like perverted R. Kelly who loves screwing little girls or boys and does prescription pills with dope, you get off scot-free, leaving the victims hurting with no way to cope. They're not talking about how sex prostitution is legal in Amsterdam and is one of the major areas for sex trafficking. They're trying to legalize it here in America as well, but nobody is talking about that. They're not talking about the married individuals who cheat with every Tom, Dick, and Trina in between the sheets. They forgot to mention themselves or those who sell and commit death in the streets. They're not concerned about those who've committed fraud or stolen things here at home or abroad. They aren't concerned about the pedophile who took the little girl's innocence as her parents took payoffs while the rest of her family lay asleep. They were not praying or speaking on the men who misled but also fucked their flock of sheep. I'm sick of hearing "pray the gay away" when it's some much more important shit going on in the fucked-up world every day. They need to remember to pray for the whores and all the pretenders because no one is perfect. They sit around with their noses turned up to the sky, holy oil in hand judging others as if they're God. The so-called saints are acting like their everything but a sinner.

Whether "Saved And Delivered" way back when or now, they have no room to be tearing the next person down. "Judge Ye Not Unless Thou Be Judged". Folks are so busy condemning or prejudging others that they forget first to make sure their own damn hands are clean. I'm tired of people and their inconsiderate opinions of others. Half of them that claim to have such a huge problem is really undercover. While he was busy judging me, another woman was busy having sex with his so-called straight sister, niece, or mother. These critics or people I'm currently speaking of are some characters. God must have a sense of humor. I watch the pot calling the kettle black so many times in life also on social media, which rules the lives of many. They criticize others for going through the same situations or things they're hiding behind the internet and closed doors. If only the walls could talk. If only people really knew the truth, they wouldn't fall for the bullshit or believe the hype. They wouldn't have so much time on their hands or be concerned so much with others if they actually had a life. They judge others for being true to who they really are, but out here doing everything under the sun for likes, attention, thrills, drugs, or some money. I think it's wrong to bash others because they chose to live a life that some obviously can't understand. I'm not ignorant like that though I accept people for who they are. It's none of my business how they live or who they lay up with. Nor is it the business of those who seem to have so many opinions of them. I shall not make things that don't concern me a burden when we all already have enough crosses of our own to bear. In my eyes, no sin is greater than any other. The last time I checked, the Lord never approved of that. The way I see it being gay isn't any worse than being a child molester, rapist, racist, liar, thief, thot, womanizer, con artist, killer, a child who disrespects their parents, false prophets, etc. All those things are wrong according to the word of God. We all have a choice of deciding to do what we think is right, just like we all should have an understanding of what's not of his will and downright wrong. A chance and a choice are two things that we all wake up with every day. However, there are many who don't share the same thoughts as me. They're too full of hatred or whatever it is they use to excuse their behavior when it comes to others. They act so disgusted by a "Homo" preference or person of color that they prefer to have people who live that way isolated from the rest of the world, stoned to death, raped, humiliated, tormented, scrutinized, threatened, or killed. That's wrong. Why not just let them stand accountable for their choices on judgment day. A line we all have to stand in. Everybody has an opinion on the matter from the White

House, Tabernacles & Churches, grocery stores, salons, barbershops, and schools all the way down to the trap spots like the bottom or down the hill. The day President Obama approved gay marriage was the day a lot of people let the world, not just the LGBT community, know how they really feel. Even those on the down low or still in denial threw shade as well as if they aren't having thoughts that could possibly have God send them to hell. They called them all sorts of foul names. From bull dikes, homos, weirdos, and faggots to lesbians, bottom thumpers, carpet munchers, and sweet dick eating maggots.

 There's a long list of what they've been called, so many that I don't have enough time to recall them all. It's a damn shame how inconsiderate some people are when it comes down to other people feelings not just their pain. I pray for this world; it lacks empathy and sympathy, not just understanding; it isn't right. I truly believe the earth is the place where the devil and his army dwell. I think that because the world we live in makes a lot of people feel they're already living in hell. Living in the gutter, they don't think it can get any worse. Many of us have been asking for a way out of all this misery for years now, but nothing has changed, but the numbers of bodies being buried in the dirt. It's like many have grown accustomed to a way of life where all they know is the struggle, the fucked-up system, and all the constant hurt. A lot of them really don't know any better because they don't even know their own worth. The Mayor nor the media doesn't want to hear or report the truth, but a ninja-like me going tell it all straight like it is. Many may not like the things I'm saying, but I could give two fucks. I have the right to freedom of speech, and I plan on using it. This messed up world needs a voice; there are way too many unheard voices. This world needs healing, lots of prayers, a touch of happiness, compassion, love, and luck. I've had enough of all the drama, the funerals, drug addiction, abuse, stick up boys, fake dealers, the missing girls, the crooked politicians who don't care, and the dirty cops with their guns cocked loaded and on the tuck. You got people out here slaughtering their own kids, committing murder for hire, degrading themselves all over the internet for so-called fame, giving the perverts all the free porn that their nasty heart's desire. Islamic nations, Korea, Russia, and the United States are all beefing over money, oil, weapons, sex, and cheap drugs making fucked up decisions, leaving us the people behind to suffer and die in the crossfire. Innocent lives have not stopped being loss since 9/11. So many more individuals have died whether they were standing on the front lines, sent out on tour, trying to protect the homeland here in the states, or somewhere else across seas fighting the so-called enemy in Pakistan, Iraq, Libya, and Kuwait. My heart is still crying for the soldiers of Benghazi, who survived the thirteen-hour straight, brutal attack, for the ambassador Christopher Stevens, Tyrone, and the many others who unfortunately didn't make it back. Help came way too late, as usual, it was like witnessing another black hawk down or somewhat like a miracle in St. Anna. The government seems not to have anyone's back. They called for support only to be denied or ignored. Shit like that further lets me know what the leaders of this country really stand for. The CIA, the DEA, the FBI, the DA, the cops, and the judge all have some stuff with them and, for the most part, all operate and think the same. Why do you think it's easy for a man to still become Supreme judge even after being exposed as a reckless drunk who's assaulted a woman; sexually raping her then fully humiliating her for the entire world to see while the soon to be next president and all his groupies shout out to make America great again or chanting victory. They are out for self, and now so are most of us. People are doing whatever to survive; they no longer care if it's right or wrong. They're doing whatever they have to in order to be able to keep moving along. Welfare and unemployment lines are running a race with the dope man who a lot is relying on for a high, employment, and possibly money for food and a place. Social Services aren't trying to give the people who are in need of help shit. They're sitting behind their desks with their noses turned up like they better than the next as if some of them haven't received food stamps or received that TCA monthly check. Real talk. They're cutting back the stamps, already telling people exactly what can be purchased and, in some states, denying the elderly their medical needs because of a shortage in state funds when the government shut down due to people and their egos. The people receive nothing and the employees don't even receive their pay. They claim money is low but somehow still manage to produce revenue to supply the hood with the best heroin El Chapo can smuggle in and all the gang members a long list of military and law enforcement issued guns. The government is quick to supply the hood with coke or dope than they are to bring about justice, opportunities, more recreational activities for the youth, encouragement, and support for those who are homeless or are in need and having a hard time learning how to stay alive. They barely show love or give to the veterans and injured service members, nor do they really help or provide for the families of the fallen soldiers. So many are going through it even though many are too full of pride to admit it. I'm taking it upon myself to say what they won't. This world is really fucked up, and it needs a serious change, and I'm not speaking about the type President Obama was supposed to bring. I'm talking about a change from God, the real ruler of this dirty world. The one person who holds all power that controls everything and everybody. May he bless and protect all of us as we come once again standing in need of prayer. We need somebody and it damn sure isn't Hillary Clinton, Olivia Pope, Luscious Lyons, or Donald Trump's racist ass who would love to see all us black people in the woods hanging from a rope. Shit, real, we need the real great hope. If things don't quickly change, I can already predict how many more may be out here stealing, selling dick and pussy on the back page, being overworked and underpaid, or robbing Peter to pay Paul. The immigrants will be shipped back across the border, and our black asses may not have any other choice but to jump on some bus, train, or boat. People are already doing whatever, as you can see, to stay afloat. If a miracle or breakthrough doesn't arrive soon, we are doomed. I want way more out of life than this. Not only for myself but for everyone. I want to say all my people are doing good, even the ones who have no real desire to leave the hood. I want us to be able to bring an end to all of the attacks and put our energy and time into the grind so we cannot just unite together again as our ancestors desired, but to get this much needed money, and be more than what they say we can be eventually buying our blocks back...

Chapter Four

"Fuck FEMA"
FEMA Isn't Shit, Our People Drowned Like A Sunken Ship...

Today marks ten years since Hurricane Katrina came raining down on New Orleans. The day that storm hit is one that the world will remember forever, especially the people from those wards. It rained for days flooding their streets, breaking the levee again, wiping away the communities, homes, cars, businesses, and families. Everything for real, including their clothes, money, and food. Help took their time coming as if they weren't in a great state of emergency. To complicate the situation, even more, some citizens who volunteered to help in any way possible were denied. Regardless of the deadly flooded streets that many bodies were floating in, the help was still turned away. The government, in my eyes, simply didn't care and felt the black minorities could wait. By the time FEMA and the rest of the "so-called" help showed up, for many, it was already too late. I think it's messed up how poorly the President reacted to such a detrimental life-changing situation. Many lives were lost due to those inconsiderate jack asses procrastinating. Fucking innocent babies and elderly folks died suffering as they relentlessly sat on rooftops or in the flooded streets waiting. It's circumstances like this that have led many, including myself, to believe this country is full of hatred. I shed tears for all those who lost their lives and are no longer here. I cry for all the toddlers and babies who didn't make it. Truthfully, I cried for them all; it was a very sad sight to see it just didn't seem normal or natural. The fact that those in higher positions of power thought so little of that state and all the residents residing there was sickening. To them, it was just one less nigger they had to be concerned about. The people were devastated, so was I, but Bush and others rejoiced each day the storm took lives. While individuals were trying to climb to safety or swim free, others were gasping for air, trying their best to hold onto something for dear life until their oxygen tank was completely empty. They just sat there looking on, denying those who could've, would've, and wanted to help as the lifeless bodies flowed through the streets like dead fish in the sea. They were given no relief, help, or real sympathy. Why? It wasn't them, or theirs stuck in troubled waters. If it had of been, they would've wasted no time giving emergency aid and other types of demands and orders. What happened that day was very tragic, unexpected, and heartbreaking. I couldn't believe my eyes; the rain, the death toll, the destruction, and neglect all took me by surprise. I'm still in a state of shock and awe after all these years especially because they still don't care not just because of the decayed rotten forgotten bodies that still lay there buried under the gravel cement and dirt but because real help never came and many lives were loss as a result. They can bury our bones, but they can't bury the truth. I wished like hell that the rain would just stop, but the more I prayed, I saw more bodies being swallowed up by every drop. All those people slowly drowned, trying to hold on to every ounce of strength in them that they had left. That horrific sight was truly hurtful to watch. Babies going without diapers and formula parents can't provide the things their kids need or for themselves. The elderly and disabled really got the ass end of the table. A woman that reminded me of my grandmother died wading through the water in her wheelchair. I couldn't believe my eyes; I couldn't do anything but keep praying and crying. Those going through the deadly storm had the strength and courage while those watching were broken, waiting, and hoping. I'm amazed at just how strong my people can be even when swimming with water higher than ten feet, starving, wet and cold doing all you can to take your mind off the waves, the thunder, and the misery. They held it together, but that doesn't mean the president and others couldn't have and should have done better. I was hurting for them. Several times I had to walk away, pop open my bottle of liquor, and take several shots. Those kid's faces read nothing but fear. They died alongside many of their loved ones hoping and praying that help was near. Some people are still hoping and praying after all this time that has passed. FEMA didn't do those people right at all. I have no problem stating the fact or making their negligence clear. The lives of the people of Louisiana will forever be changed no matter the new houses being rebuild or the damaged roads that have been repaved. The hurt that stunned them all that day during Katrina has remained the same. People are still trying to learn how to move on, forgetting what happened, and coping with all the loss they've taken along with the excruciating pain. My soul cries out for them still today, just as it did ten years ago. I wish I had been in a position to lend a helping hand. I personally was devastated by watching the deadly storm and repercussions of it on the news. It was truly a horrible sight to see. I thank God every day that wasn't my family and me. Had that been Maryland, we would have all been swept away like dead fish in the Red Sea. Grace kept us from having to endure such tragedy; still, I felt what the people of New Orleans did as I watched what seemed like a horror movie on television. I'm thankful for mercy for being wrapped in his loving, protective arms. While some took it as a joke, they should've been considering themselves blessed; they weren't the ones being wiped away in the storm. Anybody that has a heart or conscience, I believe, personally was affected by it. As the world sat on the outside, looking in the media made sure they broadcasted the tragic event as much as they could. They love rubbing shit in our faces. A part of me believes the media and the new cast finds joy in reporting all the death, poverty, chaos, and tragedy they see in most of our neighborhoods. They rarely report anything pertaining to those of color; that's good. For some fucked up reason, I believe seeing certain people whether they may be Blacks or not hurting and in some sort of pain brings them great pleasure. They love to see us suffer, sometimes inflicting the torture themselves by stooping to very low and evil measures.

Some say the levee wasn't destroyed by a storm, but it was broken by the man we will never know the truth just like I will never understand how can something like that be anyone's plan. I guess it's due to the fact our hardships and misfortunes make them feel superior. It makes them feel they're freely entertained. They laugh at us, but truth be told they couldn't walk a mile in our shoes. Shit crazy but not to those in Washington DC.

 All I could do was cry and give thanks to God that because of mercy, the flood didn't wipe away my family or me. Seeing that honestly made me appreciate life even more. It's made me value all the things or people I once took for granted. Seeing all those people in the Dome saddened me to a great extent. The horrible circumstances that they were in also opened my eyes wide, letting me know that at any time and any place, death could be knocking on anyone's door. No one is exempt when the reaper comes. Their pain and praise throughout the adversity have made me a more grateful individual than I once was. I'm grateful that my life has been covered. I'm grateful it's been washed in his blood. I'm thankful for having a sound foundation to lay my head in because it could've been my home that caved in. It could've been my family, and I stuck up in an attic somewhere scared to death, cold, wet, and starving. I thank God that those bodies that lay rotten and were never found weren't me because their loved ones never got to say goodbye find closure or even have them be properly buried. A lot of people were left behind and neglected, but the media just didn't advertise it. Certain shit they feel the public shouldn't know about or see. Crazy right? They pretend those corpses aren't still there. They act as if they can't smell the foul odor of death that seeps through the air. They just crushed them up in the junk piles with the rest of the remains and debris when they called themselves starting to repair. God bless the souls that were never found. God bless the souls that felt those people didn't deserve a proper burial in the ground and closure for their family. This country isn't about shit. I'm somewhat ashamed to tell a foreigner that I come from here. George W. Bush didn't care about the people of New Orleans no more than he cared about those in New York and Washington, D.C. This bastard was chilling on his damn ranch nowhere near concerned about giving the people his support. On 9/11, his sneaky ass wasn't worried either. While the terrorists came armed and trained to kill, G.W. sat safely reading books to little children at a school. How ironic, acting oblivious as if he had no idea shit had gotten real. HE KNEW YEARS BEFORE THAT DAY ARRIVED AND THIS IS A KNOWN FACT. The former President had long been aware of the plot against the United States, even Putin and Russia tried to give a warning unfortunately that important information was never revealed or taken heed to until long afterward. In many ways, he's also responsible for all the innocent people the terrorist decided to kill. It could've possibly been prevented, but Bush obviously had other plans. I mean, after all, Osama Bin Laden and his family were not really enemies of his they were more like allies, like his right-hand man. They bash Barack and accuse him of having ties or being a Muslim, but this motherfucker befriended the same group of individuals who came blazing at us Americans with more than a loaded gun. FEMA isn't shit, and neither is he. Truth be told, George Bush senior and junior have been business partners with many terrorists for many years. They're actually allies of the once upon a time public enemy number one. Over in the foreign sands, they spent years making all kinds of deals. They try to keep that type of shit a secret, but because I'm a great reader, by opening up a book and not just my eyes, their dirty laundry was revealed. Junior's first oil company was funded with Osama's blood money. They're all dirty as shit. Bin Laden supplied at least six known states in the US with the finest Heroin a dope fiend had ever seen, and Bush allowed him to do so for years just like the government did in the past with Larry, Ricky Ross, Pablo Escobar, and currently El Chapo Guzman. At an early age, young Bush was already in the business of making deals, and they never stopped. Greed is a motherfucker! Bush, just like Reagan and Nixon, sold his own country out for cheap blow, oil, and money. For the love of a dollar, people will do any damn thing. Politicians are no different than your average joe. They're the biggest crooks if you ask me. For a dollar or a vote, those rich, white, arrogant con artists get down and dirty too. Shit, look how they got away with taking the life of Malcolm X, Martin Luther King, and JFK. They all took a hit, and the real people responsible for their murders were never charged with it. A hit that was taken out because of the C.I.A ordered the shit. An undercover faggot to be exact. I don't want to leave that out, they've already spent years trying too. They covered up a lot of the director's skeletons and burned the rest. J. Edgar Hoover is just another example that the Government isn't saints, nor do they really practice all the bullshit they're yapping about during those phony speeches they give. The white collard individuals commit more crime than your average felon who just can't seem to stay out of prison. They just aren't held accountable like the rest of us due to their position of power.

They abuse their titles, badges, and our rights as well, don't forget. Prime example: instead of taking crews out to try to save some of the people caught in the deadly storm, they were too busy harassing and arresting folks and putting them in cages like animals. They were left to rest on a thin cold sheet of metal in a jail cell or in a dorm. So many people wanted to reach out and help willing to supply whatever form of transportation, whether it be boat, car, or plane, but they were denied. FEMA didn't listen, but I and the rest of the world saw all the tears. We watched all the bodies float away. We felt their hunger. We wholeheartedly wanted to provide food, shelter, clothes, and clean water.

They didn't have anything a human would need. We wanted to comfort them. We wanted to help heal the open wounds. We really wanted help to come for those people. I found myself praying every five minutes that their help was coming soon. We heard the preachers and elderly prayer warriors as they shouted out their prayers. We heard the cries of the people who lost their homes. They lost everything but their own backbone. I admire their strength because being in a situation like that, I know it had to be very easy just to say fuck hope and give in, but they didn't. So many died waiting that day. When it comes to the death toll, the sorry-ass government had nothing but a bunch of excuses to say. Our survival to them is a game. They love to see us out in the wild, struggling to try to make a way.

Blacks being hurt or humiliated has always been their personal entertainment. When Katrina came pouring down with lightning flashing from the sky, their response to our pain was no different. They laughed at the monkeys who couldn't swim. They ignored all those people calling out for help. They didn't give a fuck at all simply because of the color of their skin and the fact that the shit wasn't happening to them. Help never came, and when they did for so many, it was already way too late. Instead of trying to do all they could, they just sat back comfortably in their warm homes and the White House looking from afar talking about "I hope they don't make it to tomorrow." One less black motherfucker they have to be concerned about. One less hungry mouth they have to feed. One less person they have to provide shelter. One less person on welfare. One less person on Medicaid because back then, there was no Obama care. One less animal to arrest on the streets. One less liability they have to pay for. One less nigger walking around with a gun. One less person they have to provide aid for or fund. One less colored individual allowed to vote. One less junkie they don't have to arrest for possession of dope. One less person they have to bag and send to the coroner. One less drug dealer they have to worry about hanging on the corner. One less elderly person to provide medication for. One less person they have to worry about begging for a free handout under the bridges or in front of stores. One less person they have to worry about being accused of killing. One less person to cry victim making the so-called good guys look like villains. One less person to have to put up in a house or in section 8. One less person they have to worry about standing in a pantry line in need of food because they have nothing to put on their families' plate. One less person that they have to enslave or imprison. One less person they couldn't care less about being among the land of the living. One less person they don't have to prejudge and then later worry about if they'll be forgiven. One less person they have to worry about spending their "Tax Dollars" to provide mental health care because they've seemed to have lost their mind. One less troubled child, they have to be concerned about being left behind. One less dealer handing out testers to the fiends in the free pills line. One less gang banger accidentally shooting up the block or slanging rocks. The levee was broken intentionally to wipe more of us out in large numbers. I said all that because you know even before that day of the hurricane, they categorized all black folks to be needy, lazy, ignorant, and troublesome. Ten years later, they're still thinking of us and treating us the same fucked up way. That's how the world is that we live in, especially when you're African American. It isn't easy being black or broke. To them our lives will never matter every death or prison filled with one of ours will always be a joke. Sometimes I feel like the southern rapper Pastor Troy when he said he was about to move to Mars because this world is a complete mess. God help us all...

Chapter Five

"Our Troubled Youth"
We Must Save Our Babies We're Losing
Them Like Crazy...

Dear God,
I pray for this generation because the only place I see is most of them headed to rehab, a prison cell, an early grave, or basically down a road of nothing but pure disaster and destruction other than being the next target on the cops must be killed next list. Way too many are troubled, hard-headed as hell, misguided, selfish, disrespectful, obnoxious, arrogant, cocky, and wild. All they know is popping prescription pills, drinking lean, going live, acting a fool, swag, staying lit, the latest cell phone or social site, new apps, keeping up with the latest trend, using all types of drugs, or having unprotected sex. Way too many of our youth are repeatedly getting into all kinds of trouble. Lacking true leadership also fathers, many are gang banging while the rest seem to be suffering from different types of addiction and depression. They need to be saved from themselves, the system, and these mean streets. A lot of them are seriously caught up or being easily influenced by all the drug user music videos and everything else that's negative for them in between. Dropping out of school to hang on the corner is at a high rate; they need to be taking advantage of all the education they can we were deprived before, and we never know which day may be too late-life changes daily drastically. Sexually transmitted diseases are real, so are the Herpes and HIV virus. It's risky and dangerous, which makes it's an issue for

the young and old to be sleeping around without precautions. They're not concerned about going to jail, not until that pressure drop on them anyway. They're not concerned about bills or making sure they have food to eat or a proper place to sleep. They don't understand anything but ignorance. They don't understand the importance of education. Shit, from the way some of them act, I don't think they value anything but molly and a quick dollar. A lot of the old heads are also on that same bullshit too. We all need to do better. Truth be told, when I sit and think about it, many of us lack self-worth, and we value all the wrong things. We buy stuff we don't need because we enjoy the attention it brings. Some people would rather have attention than respect, especially when they aren't used to getting it. We often live beyond our means fronting for folks who don't really matter or really don't give a damn, doing whatever just to be noticed. Doing whatever because we feel the need to be loved, accepted, seen, validated, and approved. We do shit we normally wouldn't or that we know is wrong just to impress another motherfucker that could not care less. It's 2016, and many people still can't see past themselves. Sitting on a high horse like they're better than everybody else knowing damn well, they really don't have a pot to piss in neither. The whole world struggles at times, and that's a fact. You can be filthy rich and still be broke. Life lessons taught me that. Money only means something to people who aren't used to having anything and don't appreciate anything. You can tell the ones who aren't used to shit by the way they conduct themselves and by the shit they're impressed by. When you sit with winners, with leaders, with go-getters, the conversation will always be different. They make it so easy to be separated from the rest. They post their entire life and all they've acquired on social media for the world to see and then have the nerve to try to call somebody nosey. This generation lives for followers, a bunch of likes, and they will post anything, most times pretending to be something they aren't.

Shit, social media got them thinking they're really celebrities or about that life. On Facebook and Instagram, everybody's a gangster, a nurse going to school, the next kingpin or queen pin, a stripper, a model, a hustler, a player, or a thot. On these social sites, people claim to be everything that they're really not. People really aren't who and what they often post — a bunch of frauds for real. I don't place everyone who uses those sites in this category, but there are many who are fronting for Facebook and Instagram doing the most. Or doing dirt, cheating, or demeaning themselves on Snapchat. Male and female. Young and old. The weak and the lame. The strong-minded ones and the bold. A mixing bowl of a little bit of everything. Shit crazy. I'm really concerned about how many of our youth are caught up in gangs. I also find it ridiculous how many lives have been lost because of it. For some stupid reason, bangers have a tendency to believe that crime pays.

 They believe being down is a part of the American way. Thanks to leaks in the government, Colombia, and Russia, our kids are out here selling drugs and guns that they aren't even old enough to legally purchase hell; some can barely pronounce the names or correct spelling of the items. Dozens of schools are closing in the black community, but more prisons are being built daily. I thought education was more important than dividing and incarcerating. It's clear they want us to fail. I also blame those who do dumb shit and send themselves to an early grave or jail. They're out here dealing stealing and killing in hopes to be popular or to make a couple million. So many men and young black boys have died on the streets of Baltimore City, Detroit, California, and Chicago. More than the soldiers have in Vietnam. Violence has become a part of daily life for many of the children who reside in the inner city. Shit, it's also somewhat the same case for rural southern areas as well. Young blacks are fourteen times more likely to die from homicide than people of other colors, especially those who are white. It's sad that they would rather take lives or willingly risk theirs instead of occupying their time with positive things. The OG's aren't leading by example anymore; they're too busy doing stupid shit too. What's even crazier is that they act oblivious to the negative way they sometimes conduct themselves. Many of the older cats have and still are directing the youth in the wrong direction. They're using the adolescents to store, sell, and purchase drugs or guns taking charges for them or also using them for sex toys, mules, or protection. The younger ones often idealize the so-called original gangsters. Instead of taking advantage and molding them to be teachers, engineers, business owners, lawyers, bosses, or whatever their little heart's desire, we have been raising drug dealers, call girls, strippers, stick up boys, dropouts, perverts, and cold-hearted killers. Then they wonder why the younger ones end up following their lead, doing the dumb shit that they do. We showed them it was ok not to have discipline, lack of respect, morals, or the need to want to be more. We showed them it was ok to push packs, and now all they know is a quick dollar to acquire expensive attire to put on their backs. We showed them it was ok not to stay in school to not pick up a book and educate their minds or a ball mastering the sport attempting to be the best player on the field, track, or court. We showed them its ok to stand around smoking weed and cigarettes. We showed the young boys it's ok to be a womanizer. We showed the young girls it's ok just to let anybody slide up inside of her. We showed them its ok to be disobedient, lacking respect and compassion for every damn body. We showed them its ok to be a side piece or a dog who can't keep his dick in his pants. We showed them its ok to be lazy and always place blame on society. We showed them its ok to abuse prescription pills when they really don't need them to treat medical issues or some sort of depression or anxiety.

The kids are strung out and popping everything you can imagine, not just Percocet, Ecstasy, or Molly. We have shown them everything but the right way. Those who chose to be an improper influence I feel has a major part in the current issues we're having now with these troubled adolescents today. They learn from us. We have to start training these children early so that they may not lose sight of which direction to go when they grow older, eventually leaving the nest. We can't let things be the same as they've basically always been, nor can we just sit around and continue to go with the flow. We have to correct where we went wrong with them and the other ones to come so that we can raise them up to be great men and women that will make a difference but also show the future generation the right way to go. When we hear folk saying how it runs in the family or the generations, we need to say that this is where it stops; we have to break the chains we must think do and be better. We are a race of intelligence, strength, and integrity. All the negative images that are often portrayed when it comes to Blacks, Hispanics, and Muslims are not who we all really are. I want us to go back to raising doctors, nurses, chefs, actors, professors, scientists, inventors, and anything else that we desire to be.

 A lot of this current generation has not properly been raised or cared for. They're hurting. They're venting. They're tired. They're frustrated. They're mad at what it seems like the world—acting out because they've never really had anyone to be there. The sorry ass government has made their living arrangements and choice of lifestyle worst by the way they often seclude most minorities, filling their neighborhoods up with liquor stores drugs and guns poor source of education and a lack of funds. Sticking us in the trap to survive basically, off of scraps, doesn't make the situation any better. In the projects, it's always dark cloudy days and hungry nights. It's always urine along with roaches and bed bugs rolling down the hallways crowded with hustlers and junkies either getting high or engaged in a knife, gun, or fistfight. The projects have given birth to so many lost souls and savages. They came into the world with nothing, forced to watch their parents struggle. They were sitting around with sad faces because the lights were cut off, and their lives are everything but what they see on television when they are admiring the lavish lifestyles of the "Huxtables ". I believe many would do better if they had better environments and were living under different circumstances. I know some kids deliberately act out for no good reason at all. Times like that, I believe we should go back to the days when the school or neighbor gave "Big Mama" a call. You know she would tear that ass up if need be, she didn't care if it was behind closed doors or out in the middle of the streets. We need to get back to the days when parents had no problems being parents or showing discipline. Nowadays, these young parents are too busy doing them or too concerned with being their child's friend. It's nothing wrong with that; don't get me wrong, I think every parent and child should share an unbreakable bond, but that doesn't mean they shouldn't lay hands on their hard-headed behinds. I'm telling you all, a lot of these kids really need somebody to bust that ass really good and to give a fuck about them. They need somebody to show them, real love, letting them know how important they are and that we care. To have a place to lay your head and a family that supports and loves you is a blessing. A blessing that many of these kids never have and probably never will know unless things change. Home is where the heart is, and a lot of these adolescents have no stable home or have only found love in the streets, so that's where they chose to reside. I've been there I can say all these things because I used to be them. I'm not ashamed because everything I was back then made me everything that I am now. I had to go through to be a blessing to someone else. The streets, that's where most get their diploma and certifications at or go in search of one. See, in their household, shit might not be peaches and cream at all. They might not know their father. Or the loser is abusive, perverted, a junkie, an alcoholic, or doing time from constantly fucking up. Nine times out of ten, their mother probably chasing behind some no-good man strung out on dope or crack. Most likely somewhere ready to get tricked because she doesn't have any cash to pay the connect, and they no longer want to put her down on the books. Many, including myself, have been raised by our grandparents because our parents were too busy doing them even to care. Granny put in that time, love, and concern. I'm grateful for the grandparents who've ever made the decision to step up to the plate. Without them, I don't know where many, including myself as a youth, would be. Addiction to drugs, gambling, money, and sex has destroyed way too many homes, breaking families apart. I believe because of that, many of the troubled teens end up reacting negatively to all the messed-up shit they've seen. They display actions of all the negative things they've been taught. Pain is the only thing some people know. It's hard to show love or remorse if you've never been taught or experienced what those things are. Not excusing the bad behavior of our youth at times at all, I'm just saying I can feel, not just relate to where they're coming from. I've gone through lots of shit in my lifetime thus far, not just as an adult but also when I was young. I once witnessed a man's life taken by the hands of an angry, loose cannon carrying a gun. That man was my father, a cheater, a con artist, a drug addict, a liar, a trifling rolling stone. My father was a hot mess for real, but I still loved him regardless. Without him, my mom couldn't have created me alone. My dad lost his life due to creeping around with another woman laid up in her husband's home. I still can't believe he had the audacity to take me along for the ride as if

I wanted to be there while he was having sex with his girlfriend from behind. I wish he hadn't because I still have nightmares of the day he died. The way he chose to live affected my life greatly. It also left me traumatized for years. Pops wasn't living right, and because of his bad ways, he was called early to return home to glory. There's a reaction for every action, and there are consequences we have to accept after making any form of a decision, especially the bad ones. A lot of this current generation isn't living right, and if they don't learn to change their ways quickly, I can see them being on the news as the next top story. I'm seriously praying for our future because right now, they're looking like a lost cause. Lately, it's been more funerals than graduations. I find something sadly wrong with that picture. The cemetery is packed with so many of our young people who've died way too soon. Too many mothers were paying for early graves and caskets instead of birthday cakes, graduation gifts, balloons, cards, and baskets. Too many left behind mourning their loved ones who've been sent to the upper room. I'm so fucking tired of seeing R.I.P. t-shirts. I'm also tired of kids dropping out of school just to hang on the damn corner. That shit doesn't make you cool. Real parents and other forms of leaders aren't in the business of raising fools. I'm tired of seeing teens being arrested and hauled off like a bunch of hoodlums to the nearest precinct to be placed in filthy urine infested prison cell. They're locking them up at school now for even the smallest thing but acting like they don't want to bring the charges against that teacher for breaking that kid's jaw and fracturing his skull. The judicial system is fucked up and running over with our kids that they even have a television show out that is a documentary of millions of kids imprisoned and caged like animals. "Prison & Killer Kids" is what they call it. It's ridiculous how many are being locked down amongst so-called savages guaranteed to come home with a few crazy stories to tell. Some of them, for some stupid ass reason, believe going in and out of jail makes you a gangster or the shit. They think it's what's up to be a part of the game. A game that doesn't love anybody no matter your stature, place of birth, or last name. It's a must that we adults show them that there's a much better way. Fuck committing crimes because, in the long run, we already know that shit doesn't pay. The only person who gives something up is the player. Whether it may be your family, assets, money, material possessions, or even worst, your life. You're bound to lose one or the other, if not all. We have to teach them to use their minds as a weapon instead of always resorting to fighting or killing each other with Ak47's, a Nine Millimeter, 357's, Desert Eagles, and a form of Smith & Wesson. Instead of taking each other lives, we could be showing them ways to capitalize on some of life's hardest lessons. We have to love one another just as God loves. We need to show more compassion so that they may learn how to love an enemy, stranger, friend, or for the same as they do their parents, sister, or brother. All this senseless killing has got to stop. Enough blood has already been shed. We can't and shouldn't continue to be the reason why our own people are held down or somewhere left for dead. We have to teach them to uplift one another instead of keep trying to put a bullet in the person on the next block over head. I know our ancestors are disappointed, and they should be considering what we've allowed ourselves to now become. They're acting as if they don't know any better than wonder why a critic is quick to consider them just another dumb nigger. I know Coretta, Kathrine, Harriett, Fredrick, Nat, and many others who fought for us are flipping over in their graves full of disappointment, confusion, sadness, and rage. They didn't make all those sacrifices and do all that marching for our black asses to act like this. They lost their lives so that we may be free. They fought hard for our rights, equality, and prosperity. They took that beat down in Selma for our rights so we could continue to grow strong as one and one day all prosper and no longer have to fight. They spent so many years being treated unfair, taken advantage of, having endured so much strife. They endured having to settle for less and accept unbearable pain. They suffered so that we could be successful. They did so much for us; we shouldn't let their deaths be in vain. We are triumphant in spite of all the adversity. We have to maintain everything that they stood for and lost. We have to use that as motivation to ultimately gain our rightful place and respect in this land, so we don't have to go back to the place from which they claim we all came. I have no seeds, but I still want better for the kids of this world. I wish nothing but great things for every young man, woman, boy, and girl. They say we were once kings and queens I say that we still are we but, we just have to make daily changes and pray for a better tomorrow. This wasn't the dream that Martin had for his people. Belittling ourselves or killing each other will never make us equal. We should be thanking him and the rest who made sacrifices by striving to be all that we can be and more. Knowledge is power. We can do better. We can be whatever we put our minds to after all a black person did make it possible for a man to visit space and allegedly walk on the moon but also become President of the United States...

Chapter Six

"A Fucking Recession"
Times Are Hard; It Feels Like the
Great Depression...

The storm hasn't passed yet we're still going through it. I find myself asking God over and over again how much longer must we suffer? Times are hard even for the white collards the rich folks but even harder for the less fortunate. The government isn't sending out any funds or resources to help those in need. If anything, they're raising taxes and cutting back on the little bit of assistance they already give. Some states are threatening to take the food stamps program away for good, also telling people what they can and can't buy, which is just another way of them controlling us that reside in the hood. That card feeds many families monthly without it; they will not be able to eat even those who go out and beat the pavement every day to punch the clock or sell rocks. The elderly can barely afford medicine or medical treatment. In my personal opinion, the Obama care package was straight up a bunch of bullshit. The young and the old suffer from it. Instead of helping, it has only made things harder. I see many older people struggling daily to make ends meet. They're struggling the most because a lot of them are no able longer to stand on their own two feet. They can't work, and they can't get the proper help that they need either. That's because the social workers feel it's already too many freeloaders down there begging with their hands out. They treat the elderly folks very harshly; they treat the younger adults even worst. They feel they're better than those who've had to stand in that welfare line. They look at everyone who comes there as if they're just a bunch of lazy individuals who don't want to get up off their behind and work. What they feel is partially true cause there are some who prefer to be given instead of going out to get it. However, that doesn't mean everyone else doesn't really need the help to get through. My grandmother can't work, and my grandfather is deceased; she receives maybe all together six hundred in cash a month and about twenty dollars on her food supplement card. The state says her income is too high to receive more, but we all know that's some bullshit they just don't want to give her more, but every time you turn around, they got money to fund some new project or to fight a war. My grandmother can't fucking survive on that petty ass income alone. Had it not been for myself and other family members, Granny probably would've been lost her home. We hold her down because the state won't. They could do more for the elderly and for the needy, but they rather waste money on unnecessary things. They could do more for the people period, but their tight greedy ass doesn't. I hate seeing my grandmother and others having to beg them bastards. I feel like what she asks for should already be a given. My grandfather was an honorable vet; he served this sorry ass country well for many years. A hardworking man and a proud soldier who bled nothing but red, white, and blue. After serving all those tours, this what they come home too? After putting his life on the line for a country that has fought against him and his race, this is how he's repaid? It makes no sense; they make bad decisions that most times are at our expense. Shit, his lack of insurance and medical problems, I believe, are what sent him to an early grave. Had they done right by him, it's a strong possibility that his life could've been saved. This's a fucked-up world we live in I swear ran by a bunch of con artists and dirty politicians who simply don't care.

The land of the free, my ass. Everything in the United States comes with a large price tag and a fee. They tax everything but food but claim to have no money to pay teachers or extra funds for the school. To survive in this country is very costly, and you better believe the price has always been higher for individuals like me. I don't understand this twisted country or the people who run it. They care more about starting a damn war than they do our children having proper education, some clean water, and food for their stomachs. The people of Flint, Michigan, are still basically drinking filthy toxic water after all this time. Not the big businesses; however, they always ensure their living and working space is much safer, not just better. This country has invested billions of us tax payer's money to send troops overseas to dictate other people's affairs, killing innocents along with criminals stuck in a foreign land that they don't wish to be. They don't have money for the schools, recreation centers, or boys & girls clubs. There are no funds to provide shelter for the homeless, no money for cures, no cash for the minorities, or for our youth. Poverty and a lack of is the main cause of crimes being committed, but they don't get it. They've no money to provide a clean water source, employment opportunities, or skilled trade centers. They've no money for our medical needs, no money for new textbooks. Sadly, they do have funds for oil, drugs, assassinations, terrorism, alcohol, for power, for campaigns, for soliciting sex, for expensive lifestyles, for the yacht club, and for surgery to ensure younger looks. They got money for spies, and money to pay people to supply. The only reason weed in particular was legalized was to control and keep the Mexican musicians and niggers in check. Ever since back in the day, they claimed weed and the devil's music was destroying their precious "White" women and kids. I have no empathy for them because nobody was going purple or giving a fuck when it was leaving all of ours addicted or dead. It's only a problem when the stuff directly impacts them. They got money for votes, but yet they have no money to restore hope. They have currency to block certain individuals from leaving or entering the country, but when it comes to the real needs of "We The People" they never have any money. They have money to blow obviously, but none to help the less fortunate folks who're stuck living in the slums or eating scraps out of trashcans because they might be what many consider a bum. How can you produce millions for an unnecessary war but no money to fix up the poverty-stricken communities or no money to help the poor? How can you have billions to spend on building walls and organizations of hate but no money for starving sick kids who need a decent meal on their plate?

How can you spend us, taxpayers, hard-earned money to support ignorance or to construct a border, but people of Flint, Michigan, are still without clean water? I spoke of this matter before and will continue because I'm tired of those people in need being ignored. The government can supply money to plan an attack but can't help the people of their own country who has to beg for assistance daily, nor can they help the young and old individuals who're addicted to drugs, and I'm not just talking about crack. They need to be more concerned with their own instead of going over to the nation of Islam, trying to dictate the way they chose to live in their homes. It's a lot of folks right here in the states that could use the extra help, but they're always denied, or the so-called help comes way too late. They should be making sure; first, we're all straight, but that's impossible because they're greedy, inconsiderate, prejudiced, and full of hate. For years this is the creed we have been forced to live with and by. They treat us as if fucking freedom is a special gift. They act as if we should just accept whatever they throw our way and be grateful. However, maybe what was given isn't enough. Those who work still have struggles.

Those little petty checks help, but times can still be or get tough. Everybody needs somebody sometimes, so why not uplift your own instead of being concerned with foreign policies and dropping Muslim bodies. I'm starting to believe the only foundation this country is built on is discrimination, hate, and greed. I don't believe they really care about our needs. I get mad every time I think about how comfortable they live off our blood, our underpaid work, our sweat, our tears, our fears, and our hard-earned coins that the IRS took. The leaders in DC are nothing more than a group of racist money-hungry crooks. We can never change the portrait of us that society has painted if we can never receive equal opportunities, fair and just treatment, or any real support in the matters that are causing us to come up short often. We can't better ourselves divided or by sending one another to graves or to court. We have to stand united no matter what and put all the extra bullshit aside. In ourselves, in our race, in our communities, we must take more initiative; we must also take more pride. We must take these elections seriously. We have to stop thinking our votes don't matter; that's the first step of trying to have our voices heard. We have to stop being so violent when shit doesn't go our way but, at the same time, keep demanding equal pay. We have to make more use of our brain instead of sitting around waiting on a handout from social service or social security to maintain. We must mold our children and our minds to be more ambitious in spite of adversity in order to have some real money or help come across our families' hands. Even though we're in need, I want to show our babies its more to life than standing on the corner. When we do better, we can educate, motivate, and build our empires like Tom Joyner. The struggle is real; this isn't something that just became an issue; times have just gotten worst.

However, shit has been real way before the riots. We were upset way before Trayvon or before they told the movement to be quiet. Shit has been real before this recession; it's what really has half the world suffering from depression. Religion, money, drugs, and bad deals have brought us down to a low level and ripping this country apart. Shit is so hard that even those who desire to do no wrong have started doing a little dirt too just for the sake of needing extra cash to get by. Many are out here robbing Peter, the landlord, just to have enough to pay Paul for the electric bill. Many are selling themselves short for a sense of stability or for a good fix or feel. Women are out here tricking to keep the lights on and put food on their table. Men are put in a compromising position including breaking the law to put clothes on their children's backs or getting money for extra bills outside the rent like the water payment and cable. Due to this recession, people are resorting to low standards because their lives are unstable. People are tired of living from check to check, tired of being stressed out, tired of trying to figure out how they're going to make ends meet next. There are many who like to front acting uppity knowing they really don't have it. They can tell all the lies they want, though, but the struggle is real for most, just on different levels. Different situations and different reactions but the same hunger, the same pain, and the same devils. It's hard out here for us all, not just the so-called pimps when it comes to the recession, and people of color are not exempt. We need God's help to fly over this storm like the good year blimp. We need an increase. I pray for prosperity for us all. I pray even harder that our troubles in such a tough time don't last that long. We need the atmosphere to shift so we don't have to keep doing whatever to survive, so we don't have to resort to doing wrong to stay alive...

Chapter Seven

"Presidents or Optimists"
Trump Is A Bigot A Womanizer A Circus Clown. Hillary Is A Liar A Friend Of A Pedophile A Con Who Will Do Anything For The Crown...

Election time is nearing, and all the candidates are a bunch of liars, circus clowns, and jack asses. I don't believe any of the wolf tickets they try to sell us American and Foreign citizens, nor do I have faith in any of the changes they claim to make should they be elected. The country is in shambles financially, we are trillions of dollars in debt, Uncle Sam is taxing the fuck out of us taxpayers in every check. Everyone has divided not just the blacks as they say and most of the people are angry and in an uproar. They're very unhappy and frustrated for many reasons. Look at how many of us are already out rioting and protesting that the government and law enforcement refuse to change. Mad that they're struggling and can barely keep their heads above water. Mad because someone that was supposed to serve and protect unlawfully killed or imprisoned their son or daughter. We're suffering due to bad decisions they make or sneaky moves that should've never been made. It's too many crooked politicians in the

White House, Congress, Senate, and the courts already. Most black people like myself no longer have hope in the system, and we damn sure don't trust them. Honestly speaking, we've received everything from them crooks but equality, fair pay, justice, and support. Mistreatment from them has affected us in great numbers, whether denying our children education, killing us off, not employing and canceling us, throwing us under the bus, or throwing us behind bars. The United States has more prisons than any other country, and it continues to open or build more almost every year, but the schools in mostly black impoverished neighborhoods are closing. Isn't education supposed to be more important than incarceration? There are more African American men locked up in the system or on parole pissing in the cup for probation or wearing a GPS monitored bracelet than men of color who were enslaved in the year of 1850. The DA and the judges are on their best bullshit too. There are so many Hispanics and Blacks who've been arrested for some minor charges or false ones doing life or a whole bunch of years but those dirty cops who killed 990 people to be exact in the year of 2015, the molesters, and the baby killers are free-roaming the streets without fear. I've yet to see really any of those officers be held accountable for the crimes we all know they committed or do time or face murder charges. They take our family members' lives, and it's just disregarded. So many innocent adults and children have been slaughtered, and all of our complaints about the issues have been ignored. They just sit in the White House and look at these victims as if they're the crooks in the wrong or just plain out retarded. If we aren't in a casket, we're locked away in a cell. 1 out of 14 black boys and men are serving time, and 1 out of 7 are on probation or parole in New Orleans specifically, but there are thousands of pedophiles and murderers living free in society. Shit like this needs to be addressed, but it hasn't, and I doubt it ever will. As the candidates go out making speeches and selling a bunch of lies from state to state, they've forgotten to focus on the really important issues at hand. Donald declares he will destroy ISIS within the first thirty days of power if he should win the seat. That concerns me, but he doesn't care about more innocent lives being placed in harm's way or in the dirt six feet deep. This guy's mouth is reckless, and so is his demeanor.

He's very unethical and a corrupt dirt bag. Each and every one of the candidates running in my eyes is nothing but lying snakes with their true colors along with their foul intentions written all over their faces. We can't trust any of them or their kind. Instead of focusing on the severe needs of the people, they're too busy scheming and exciting the crowds with their plans to go bomb foreign grounds. While Trump is running around making deals with Russia to win, Hillary is leaking sensitive information too. Then they wonder why we're so upset. The problems within the country are steadily increasing but also still being ignored or brushed off, and none of them are speaking of ways to make a difference; they're just making shit worse for themselves and us. Out causing more issues but putting the troubles here at home on the back shelf. The people who support him and his opponent don't view stuff the same way as we do. Just like back in the day when we had to boycott because we were tired of having to walk or ride the back of the bus. They can come up with new ways to destroy us but not to bring a resolution to make life better also safer for all. They don't care about the way blacks Hispanics and Muslims are made to live just as none of them gives a fuck about these heartless bastards out here molesting and killing kids. Here is a prime example; a man was arrested for two joints of marijuana and was given a 13-year sentence while Casey Anthony, on the other hand, killed her daughter the judge found her not guilty when we all know that bitch did it.

Death sentences are being handed out to drug dealers, but they're setting free baby killers. Unjust circumstances such as this are one of the many things that should be getting addressed, but at the end of the day, none of this affects them directly so they couldn't care less. I don't believe I saw her heartless ass shed one tear, and it has been beyond easy for her to up and move on. Her ass needs to be in jail, but the system has their picks and is often on some other nonsense. This needs to be changed, but it won't. The politicians and the judicial system are both corrupt. White people and law enforcement break just as many laws, if not more, but when it comes to equality and justice, their situation is always handled differently. Eight hundred seventy-five people have been shot and killed thus far this year in the United States, and not a damn thing has really been done about it. Most times, the judge and police chief never give a fuck. If you're a person of color automatically, they assume you're guilty. More than 700,000 black men are confined to a cell, which makes some further believe they designed the judicial system in hopes of ensuring another way for us to fail. The officials up in the higher positions aren't doing anything to resolve this long ongoing issue. They act oblivious. They act like they really don't care. It doesn't bother them that they treat us unfairly. Instead of putting the people first, they're too busy trying to figure out a way to stay or become a millionaire. Too busy trying to figure out a way to be the next headwoman or man in charge. We're their last priority, why do you think the country is in debt and struggling the way it is? They're too concerned with running schemes, destroying this nation, and killing the supposed to be the American dream. They're not trying to make anything better that's just the lies they tell, so in the elections, they will prevail. I see right through all their bullshit, though. I'm no fool. The only thing they're talking about is putting us in further danger and ways to completely take over for real. Police brutality, gang killings, poisonous water problems, and the economy, in general, are their last thoughts. Education is very important, so is no child being left behind, but I hear no plans being discussed during the speeches as for the low salary payment teachers receive or how their pay is constantly being cut. I haven't heard anything about the lack of funds to provide the proper education our youth needs or how they plan to decrease the closing of schools, many of which are in black and impoverished environments.

They haven't discussed the massacre in Chicago or how the Vice Lords and Gangsters Disciples are dropping more bodies than Isis. They're now calling the windy city Chiraq. Morticians are getting rich, hundreds of black boys and men are being found in a ditch, hundreds of mothers going crazy in tears because their babies have been shot down like they weren't shit. Donald hasn't spoken on this particular matter because he loves to see one of us get hit. The vulgar, disrespectful, racist, womanizer can't stand blacks either. We hurt when we see one of ours being taken away, but he and the clan love it. They wish death to all of the "Niggers ". The KKK will be bursting with joy if one of their leaders was to win that presidential seat. I can see them dressed in all white rags and torn sheets armed with heavy artillery ready to take over DC and every other street. They better be prepared for a fight though if they do try it, we aren't our grandparents, and we will not just bow down or be quiet. We will be handing out ass whippings of our own, and I promise you it will be much worse than when they claim we're acting aggressive or instigating a riot. Not making threats at all just saying what's real. We're not going back in chains, nor will we be treated like animals or out slaving in their cotton fields. If both of their racist asses knew what was best, they would try to find a way to unite the country instead of wanting it to stay divided. Chaos will be the only outcome because shit never works out even when it's lopsided. I believe chaos is what they both want, though. If you've been listening carefully to their speeches, they've practically already told you so. I don't hear anything about real change, nor when it comes to their many plans, I don't see where any of it will really be making a difference. The real issues are being ignored; I said it once, and I'm going to say it again. I will keep speaking my mind until I see real change happening. They should be concerned about global warming, but now they're making deals with foreigners, whether it may be for drugs, oil, or weapons of mass destruction that Korea and Russia claim they've never seen. Hillary Clinton, under the microscope, is doing dumb shit and being sneaky, further tarnishing her campaign and her last name as if her husband hasn't already fucked that up enough with rape charges and his side piece Monica Lewinsky sending his presidential position straight to hell. Not to mention the country can't seem to forget how much he loved to smoke weed and get his penis sucked. He should've kept that thirsty hoe out the house and his penis on the tuck. All their dirty laundry could be a reason her chances of winning are fucked. Hillary talks a good game, but when you think about it, most of those officials are all the same. They have the gift of gab, but they don't fight for the people, they use us as pawns or test dummies in one of their secret labs. They aren't for the citizens of this country; they're just in it for the fortune, the fame, the power, and of course, the money. They've got many skeletons that only get exposed when their friends run against them. Snakeskin starts showing, and claws are out why do you think Jeffery Epstein was silenced well basically wiped out. What was once good times together is no longer fun and games. The shade is thrown, pictures are shown, wired taps are put on their opponent's phones. Donald and Hillary, in my eyes, are more scandalous than Olivia Pope or a junkie on dope. The two are truly two of the same kind. Crooked politicians like them are the main reason, so many of us have gotten left behind. Before in my younger days, I used to think that maybe some of us were lazy and that the Bush family was crazy (Still Believe That to This Day), but now I realize they just haven't really given us much opportunity. They've given us more hardships and obstacles than they've given us an equal chance, creating more room for all of us to advance. The government really isn't shit, especially when you count all the lives loss and all our tax money spent. I can only imagine how things will be if that asshole with the bad toupee persuades the people better than Hillary. That ignorant racist prick isn't a reliable and reasonable person on whom we can depend. Mind you; he has filed for corporate bankruptcy more than four times in just eighteen years. It's obvious when it comes to money and power; he isn't responsible or trustworthy. He's ripped many people off after creating a fake college where thousands of tuitions had actually been paid. The media doesn't like to air that type of news out for the world to see through, but I will. I'm very concerned about the wellbeing of my people but also this entire country. He will put us all in great danger; he has already made that clear during almost every speech so far. With him, in the office, we can definitely count on crying over many more Trayvon's or Dontre Hamilton's. Donald Trump, in my personal opinion, is dumb as shit for real, and he has no type of experience when it comes to politics. When asked an important question or how he will change the world old boy don't have a fucking clue how to answer. He's spent most of his campaign so far just bashing his opponent like he isn't dirty too. Crazy, but I'm glad because this just gives us an early taste of the shenanigans he's probably going to do. Trump hasn't spoken much at all when it concerns the wellbeing, injustice, and safety of the people. Instead, he just says something else stupid, avoiding the question and pretending it's just his way of showing he has a sense of humor. If he wins this presidential election, we the people are most certainly done. Observing the speeches as they continue to campaign, I believe his ability to run an entire country is more than likely probably slim to none. I'm still trying to figure out how in the heck he felt he has the credentials and qualifications to run. Having a certain amount of money doesn't mean you qualify, or at least I thought, but then when I really sit back and think about it, most elections and powerful positions have been bought. Trump is so full of shit but got the nerve to try to discredit the first black president? Obama isn't perfect; he's human. Some people are way too hard on him. They act like they can't remember George W. Bush left all this turmoil, destruction, and millions of other issues on him from the beginning, including debt to mend. Barack promised change; he didn't promise us a damn miracle. They expected him to do only what God can. I'm personally grateful he extended our rights if nothing else. People complain, but it could be a lot worse, like how life will be if Trump's trifling ass got elected. For them to have expected some magical change to occur in eight years after being fucked up for sixteen straight and by a "Black Man, " I find that to be very hysterical especially after all the years many of them have gone out their way to down play us, never giving us credit, and considering us lazy bastards. Those racist white folks and politicians are seriously a mess, but then they wonder why the people are under so much duress. Even some of the white collared Democrats are feeling the stress. The problem with the struggle and the judicial system is real. Blood is being shed worldwide. Seeing the way stuff is now, I'm starting to think like my grandparents when they say this world is soon coming to an end. I hope we've all gotten it together before the trumpets begin. I'm hoping for that great change to really come back everywhere, not just here in my city. I pray for peace and prosperity. We are so much more than the dope strips that the government sent heroin to. We're more than the crack houses and liquor stores. We're more than the dead bodies in the park that the media go out of their way for outsiders to see. We're more than the thugs, losers, and drug abusers the Mayor and other officials who spectate have labeled us as. They put us down more than they use their power to uplift. We're more than every negative word they sit around and critic us with. We just have to get back to actually believing it. We have to care more about ourselves since the government shows us constantly that they don't. It's hard to be black, but it's even harder to be black and concerned and still be considered an American. We have to do what we can to better our current situation even if they refuse to or just won't. If they don't want to change, then we have to make them by any means. Not trying to instigate a riot or anything negative just saying we need to take power over our lives and wellbeing back. We have to grind harder like Nino Brown had G money and the rest of the workers slaving at the Carter. We need to invest in ourselves more, in our kid's futures, and business establishments. Bring the money and employment back to our people, fuck keep spending our last at Walmart, Footlocker, Ralph Lauren, and Michael Khors to some racist folks who don't respect or see us as their equals. We need to buy up all the land, oil rigs, franchise restaurants, malls, and every store. It's obvious our lives are no longer safe in their hands, and we can't keep wasting precious time that isn't guaranteed; we must now come up with a master plan. It's time we remember the kings and queens we once were and still are. We need to adjust our crowns and regain the upper hand. We can't wait on them to send in the help. The people of New Orleans are still waiting on FEMA to cut a check. We have to find our own hustle and make them understand. We are not going to tolerate the bullshit anymore. We will not just continue to bow down, struggle, suffer, wither away, and die. We're not asking; we're going out and taking the opportunity to better our lives and those around us. We're going to get this money, grow strong together as one, prosper, stay prayed up, and expand. The government, as a whole, has let us down and have been doing so for years. Their messed-up ways have many, including some whites living stressed and in fear. People have become desperate if not hopeless and heartless. I really don't foresee shit getting any better either look at the two candidates who will eventually have total control over this land. We're damned if Clinton wins, and we're damned if she doesn't know this, some people have already made the decision not to vote. I'm afraid; personally, I'm not trying to be back shackled down deported away on some white rich person's boat. Fuck that I promise you I will be the first one to be killed or to go afloat. We've definitely got to find a way to make the situation work. Starting today, we need to depend less on them for help and learn to put ourselves first. Soon there will be no more resources for minorities to get help. This isn't facts as of right now, but I'm more than certain we can look forward to one day these things will no longer be there. They're stripping us already of everything bit by bit. They don't want us to have anything that may be a benefit. After this costly election, shit will be worse, and people won't have extra money for vacations, new cars, and homes or a new pair of shoes or a purse. Pockets are damn near on empty now, but we won't have anything but lint in them if Trump walks away with the crown. Prices for everything are about to be raised sky high instead of going down. Honestly speaking, neither one will probably do right by us, so we should start saving up every extra dollar that comes around. This scumbag might do the unthinkable in his first week and have all of our asses Africa, Canada, Iraq, Pakistan, Afghanistan, or Europe bound. Not trying to predict the worst, I just know how these no-good crooks operate; they have the eyes of the devil and move like a snake. We can't just continue to sit around and let them be the dictators of our future or our fate. Shit, I'm just trying to protect myself and let others know what's real before it's too late. People can be smart and take heed of the free information and knowledge I'm trying to give them because I know that's what our race needs. The truth, motivation, inspiration, hope, and encouragement. I got love for my people. I want to do my part to make a difference, fuck relying on the next president. This book could be a blessing in disguise. I speak words that have been Heaven sent. I want more for us all, even if the Republicans or even the democrats don't. I want to stress the need for and the importance of educating our minds. I don't want to continue to see dropouts, dead bodies, or unfortunate folks left behind. I express the importance of a legal hustle to ensure stability but also to decrease the chances of them having a petty reason to touch you. I want us to stop being crabs in a bucket. We all need each other to survive in this cold world where when it comes to our lives and wellbeing the enemy, opposition, and the government have continued over and over again to ignore our cries and concerns, slept peacefully in the comfort of their homes, or office and said fuck it. We have to stand together because we're so much more powerful untied as one. They've always tried to keep us divided because they really fear that. Look how they reacted when Huey Newton and the black panthers or Nat Turner, Hawk, and the rest of the slaves who had the courage to step up put their evil asses flat out on their backs. Separation and confusion, along with hatred amongst one another, just make it easier for those who wish death upon us to attack. We have to be smarter; it's a must. We can't continue to allow them to make fools of us. We have to make wiser decisions, cautiously deciding every move like you would in a game of chess. Calculating every step and always planning for the future will enable us to maintain a stable life with or without their help. I've learned the decisions we make now dictate the outcome later sometimes when we least expect it too. So, I say fuck waiting, or depending on the government or others; it's time for us to get back to doing for ourselves because, at the end of every day, we always have that if nothing else...

Chapter Eight

"Crazy Debate In A Nation Full Of Hate"
A Liar, A Rapist, A Murderer, And A
Racist...

Donald Trump or should I say Donald Dumb has a very reckless mouth that he seriously doesn't know what to say out of it. If people were really smart, they wouldn't vote for the ignorant prick, although I know Hillary isn't much better. However, this cat has issues that will eventually become ours if we don't choose wisely. I wish those who haven't been following the debate could hear some of the ignorant shit he's had to say. Matter fact, I'm going to enlighten them. For starters, just to let you know what type of mind frame he really has, he proudly said, "Ariana Huffington is unattractive both inside and out. I fully understand why her former husband left her for a man. He made a good decision. "He also boastfully said, "One of the key problems today is that politics is such a disgrace that good people don't go into government. This was the exact words of the horse himself. Oh, let me share this quote. I want to mention this one for sure being that I can't focus on them all; it's way too many." "When Mexico sends its people, they're not sending their best they're sending people that have lots of problems; they're bringing crime, and they're rapists." This describes him and everyone else in DC, yet that's what he had to say in reference to Mexicans. I could recite so many more of his quotes, but I won't. I think I've been able to make my point clear that he's a joke. I could never be a part of this campaign. His words hold absolutely no value with me. I'm far from impressed with the shenanigans I've been watching on television. From what I've seen thus far, he's been talking really crazy during every presidential campaign debate. God must really have a sense of humor to create a piece of shit like him. That guy is really ignorant and a funny character. I don't understand what makes him think he will be the people's choice unless they're crazy. I don't know many people will put a black circle beside his name. He swears he's slicker than an oil spill, but he sounds illiterate and clueless each time he's asked a question. He's just another idiot with money; I don't take the clown seriously at all. Trump is just like many other racist white, rich man who believes he will always be above the law. This election is really a joke to Donald, the redneck that pay minors to fuck.

When it comes to the wellbeing of the people of the country, he really doesn't give a care. He's just doing this because he knows he can. His running period and actually being voted for is evidence that money can buy you power. I personally believe every ballot that has or will be stamped with his name on it was done due to many others like him being prejudice and, of course, the almighty green dollar. I pray hard he doesn't win the election, but that day will be here before we know it. Obama's last term doesn't seem to be ending so well. There's a video surfacing around of him allegedly showing his erection to female news reporters on Air Force One. Donald and his team have stooped to the lowest levels to make him and his opponent Hillary Clinton look bad. Thanks to the negative opinion of Trump and others, Barack's chance of still being the people's choice may be shot all the way to hell. They feel his way of running the country hasn't met their approval still or isn't up to their standards.

They ruled against every idea he came up with, whether it benefited us or not. The Republican party has made it very clear that they can't stand the President, and they've been going in on him down Capitol Hill. President Barack says he was trying to make moves; he also wants to make business deals. His opposition isn't trying to hear anything he has to say, though. They could give two fucks about his opinion or appeals. During the time of both his terms, they've criticized him terribly, blaming him for Bush's major fuck ups. They're spreading rumors that he's actually a Muslim who has ties with terrorists along with many other things a person can imagine. I think they have him confused with the former Presidents who came sixteen years before. They're saying everything negative that they can say about Obama, including him being a weed smoking whore. They're placing him in the same category as former presidents and elected officials we all know. I personally feel Barack did his best, considering he really didn't stand a chance of fixing the mess they created from the start. The people wanted a miracle to happen that probably never will happen, not even when Jesus comes back. I believe the only reason he was voted in any way is that the economy was extremely jacked up. In a recession, at war, and a bunch of other nonsense that the public never heard about before.

So, much was already on that man's plate long before his inauguration. There were already a million discussions about how several foreign countries had nuclear weapons galore. Bush did a lot of dirt while he was in office and his father. They've done a lot of dirt in the White House, on his ranch, foreign soil, and behind many other closed doors. I'm happy to have been blessed to live to see a black person in such a high position of power. Regardless of what the haters say, he's going to make history. I try not to be so hard on the President; the damn man is human and not God. I'm just not quite sure if Obama or we the people were exactly understanding of the amount of pressure and problems that he was in store for. I say he played his hand the best he could considering what he had been dealt. The President did all that the critics and congress allowed him to do. He may have been the one sitting in the higher seat, but those crooks were still in control and running the show. They, unfortunately, had other things in mind when it came to the wellbeing of the American citizens and foreigners. They made decisions based on their own personal feelings, beliefs, and past experiences. Yet they say that's why a woman shouldn't run the country. They never really cared for a black man being the head motherfucker in charge. A lot of them secretly despise having to take orders from his "Banana Eating High Yellow Walking and Slick Smooth-Talking Ass ". They burn with rage deep inside having to follow the demands of a "Monkey ". It has messed with some of their self-esteem heavily, and it has bruised their little ego. Having to listen to him killed their pride. They really don't like his black ass. I'm surprised the C.I.A didn't put him on the list to be the next victim of a homicide. Maybe it would've happened by now if Hoover's punk behind was still living. It has never mattered to them that he's a half breed. They don't see him as being mixed. They see him as another colored bastard that they will always view as not being worth shit. Those crackers were riding in those expensive cars residing in big houses in safe neighborhoods, black suitcases, and fancy suits been wanting to have his butt thrown out the White House. They say his purpose was served during the first term they've been trying to find every reason since then to give him the boot. They consider him an animal too, just like the people we saw on the news last month running wild through liquor stores with friends, causing chaos rounding up the squad to loot. They sit around daily, judging him as if they're perfect when they know their devilish butts are nowhere near a saint. They're the ones who're a bunch of frauds pretending to be everything they think the public would want to hear or see, but they can't pull that bullshit over on me. I know way better than to believe the hype or all the stuff I hear and see on tv. All I see when I look at them is a constant reminder of the type of foul distasteful screwed up person I never want to be. They have so many tricks up their sleeves that they make lying look super easy. They call some of us troubled, ignorant, and lazy thieves, but they forgot to mention that they too are sometimes, if not most times, dishonest, greedy, not loyal, full of shit, sneaky, drug addicts, hustlers, gangsters, crazy, and sleazy. Even Hillary, Obama's right-hand woman, has some crap with her too. The old girl has gotten herself caught up in some email scandal. Of course, she denies the accusations, but Trump and the media is making that almost impossible. Mrs. Clinton has made the top of the news, and her face is plastered on every channel and website. Her facial expression looked as if she was shocked, trying to act oblivious to what she was being accused of. The former first lady had the dick look on her face like oh shit I've finally been exposed. I've been caught. They think they got me, but watch how I act clueless and beat the charge. Shorty tried her best to play dumb at first was actually mad. She claims she doesn't understand why they thought she would do some deceitful stuff like this. Lying to herself and everybody else. I believe it, but some people barely even mention it now. Crazy how things can change so quickly when you're considered a person of power and good wealth. She leaked that shit and was still allowed to run for President. Those Democrats got some shit with them as well. I'm not going to try to paint a perfect picture just because that's the party I choose. I much rather just keep it real, something they refuse to do. I'm the type to speak my mind, especially when it comes to important matters such as this, and I really don't care how it makes others feel. It's about damn time our voices started being heard. I have no cut cards. I tell a person straight up how it is. It's my personal opinion and also my right to speak the truth. I'm going to say or write what I want to period. However, I am voting for the sneaky trick Hillary. I just wanted to point out that I'm not proud of everything she and some others in her party do. All those politicians are crooked in some sort of way in my eyes. They all have misled the people one time or another. They all have fed us false hope bullshit speeches on how they plan on changing the world for the better and a bunch of other lies, guns, and highly addictive dope. We're screwed either way; that's how I personally see it regardless of who may win this crazy election. This country is messed up in debt, still making bad deals, and starting problems in other nations; just like in the movie "The Patriot" with Mel Gibson, the war will soon be in our own back yards. I'm praying hard Jesus will be a fence around me and those I love. Shit is crazy. It's as if the government won't be satisfied until Russia, Isis, or Korea comes with some heavy artillery to bust us wide open unexpectedly, hoping to teach our hardheaded asses another lesson. "White House Down ", "Olympus Has Fallen ", and "London Has Fallen" was good action-packed movies, but we won't find that situation so thrilling when it becomes a reality. Shit is real, and every time you turn around, these fools are just giving them more reasons and more ideas. I can foresee many more innocent lives being lost just like fifteen years ago during nine eleven. That was a catastrophe when the Twin Towers came crashing down, sending all those terrorists to Hell and the victims to Heaven. Until we learn to mind our own business and just take care of home and let them other countries be, they will continue to plot ways to kill us Americans off. They will continue to have some of us living in fear, poverty, and misery. If the government knew what I know, they would come to some type of agreement. God bless America and also other countries.

Those politicians are playing with our lives as much as a chef uses his sharp knives. They think with greed, hate, and envy in their hearts. Their negative way of thinking is exactly why the world is so jacked up, divided, and falling apart. They live carefree even during the so-called hard times at the expense of our hardworking taxpayers. They have access to so much money that they have absolutely no idea what to do with it. They build, they collect, they ship drugs to our neighborhoods, and they rob the poor. They send Uncle Sam at us for a piece of our cheddar while we struggle. Working underpaid, we can barely keep a roof over our heads or feed our families. Most days, it's as if we're still some white master's slave. They are living good while we are stressing from pay to pay wondering how we're going to make way for bills and for food on our tables.

Sweet land of liberty supposedly they say but how much has actually been sweet in this country for people of color or your average minority. They make moves that benefit their livelihood. They don't care if their budget cuts or tax increases can leave us all not able to live comfortably or good. To me, none of them are really for us; they're more so all about the secret family and themselves. Truthfully speaking, they really don't care about us. God is really the only higher power I trust. However, knowing all of this, I still feel like getting out there in November to vote is a must. I'll be damned if I'm trying to see us go back to the old days where we had to eat slop, piss, and poop in a pot floor or dirty hard cold ground in place of what should've been a bed or at least a damn cot. Picking cotton, messing our hands up, mending the fields, tending to the animals, training chickens to fight (Yet they try to give us life for fighting dogs as if they aren't both animals) and being forced to put up with disrespect and physical abuse while taking care of a little smart-mouthed boy named Billy and a smart-mouthed sassy little blond-haired blue-eyed girl named Lilly. Daily you are on your back when the master says so or got you down one bending knee making you feel like daddy dirty little hoe.

Hands cuffed, and he got the key putting his bastard kids in a "Nigger" woman whom he would never consider family. Splitting open our backs with whips because they say we're hard-headed niggers always acting unruly and ignorant. I don't know about anybody else but that most certainly wouldn't be the best lifestyle for me. I couldn't or wouldn't live like that. I would rather be killed first and die with dignity. I will never allow the white man or anybody else to have power over me. Fuck that! Excuse my language, I have to work on expressing myself better, but these issues at hand just have me in my feelings. I care. I feel enough pain already from what we have had to endure daily but also from my ancestors every time I read something that pertains to our history. God bless the people and God bless me. We're the endangered species now. I can't help but have so much concern for my folks and others not for just myself and my family. These presidential candidates talk a good game, but they will say and do anything for a little piece of fame. I feel our lives are worth way more they can't continue to put a cheap price on our head. How they operate in office is not what we the people stand for. I haven't heard exactly how they plan to bring about change that will actually make a damn difference yet. All they've been discussing is how scandalous, vindictive, racist, heartless, and how sneaky each other are. Election day hasn't even arrived, but I and many others can already see the disaster from afar. I have no faith in a prejudice jack ass or a liar. Before I would trust dishonest individuals like that, I would rather walk through a million rings of fire.

They're both very deceiving and manipulative. You can tell by the way they talk, the way they conduct themselves when the cameras aren't around, how they've treated others over the years, and from their poor or bad backgrounds. If they were doing dirty shit back, then it's no doubt in my mind that they won't do some crazy stuff now. They haven't changed. Not trying to come off being judgmental, I'm just trying to get them to see how they're bringing the people and the economy down. Some many lives have been lost here at home, and on the battlefields overseas, so many troops dead bodies are being shipped back home to their family. It's ridiculous how many men and women have died serving a country that doesn't care about them. They have them fighting a war in Iraq when they should be concerned about the war here in the US on people who're black...

Chapter Nine

"Chiraq"
The Streets of Chicago Feel Like The Battlefields in Iraq...

Last night, I watched an urban movie, another hit to add to Spike Lee's list of other classics; it's called "Chiraq. "It's a very good movie; however, there are some things, many things honestly speaking, that really bothered me. I must be honest in regard to how I really feel about it even though what I have to say might piss some folks off. After and while watching the movie, a part of me somewhat instantly, in some ways, felt ashamed at that very moment to be black. Surprising right? I know the thought had caught me off guard, too, because I 've always been proud of it. I love everything about the color of my skin, and that's something that I put on everything. I love all that I am and everything I do. BLACK IS BEAUTIFUL. It's just seeing the way we colored folks were being portrayed was embarrassing and nowhere near funny but mostly true. The characters were a bit extra though as far as the acting is concerned, especially Nick Cannon, he's still whack like his rap album. They picked the lamest dude ever to play that part. He's a straight-up clown he tried his hardest though. I couldn't help but laugh at him, but the overall message in the movie was heartfelt and further let me know that too many of us are dying and in large amounts due to nonsense, colors, and people who are considering themselves representing their block. Gangs are battling daily, and the preachers have had to comfort way too many parents because their kid got shot. That's ridiculous; the kids can't even be safe at the playgrounds, schools, or bus stop. The windy city is too full of hate, pain, and heartaches. Between the years 2001 and 2015 alone, 7356 people have been killed in Chiraq. Thousands of black male's dead by the hands of other black males aren't cool. That shit is actually really sad, so is seeing all these mothers crying over the babies they once had. Self-inflicted genocide is what I call it, but many, especially those out busting the guns without a care in the world, don't see it that way. Truth be told, they really believe taking each other's lives is okay. They find pleasure in all the dumb shit they do, but the victims could have done without the gunplay. Their loved ones shouldn't have had to suffer. Most importantly, why take the life of another sister or brother? Many gang members would rather get caught with a gun by the cops than to be caught slipping without one encountering a rival. The mindset of many is fucked up, and murder is their ultimate plan for survival. They need to have a change of heart and put the guns down. The people are sick of their loved ones being dead on arrival. Shit is crazy in this city, just like many other ones around the world. Young and the old are out here killing each other over colors, blocks, money, sex, pills, dope, etc. They take life with no remorse while the rest are stuck living in the slums of the trap, eventually heading nowhere; that's a good place for them to be; they're dying way too young way too fast. Many residing on the Southside and also the West are living in fear and have lost faith because of all the recklessness. I pray for Chiraq. I pray all this madness can end, and they can bring love and the real Chicago back. Their city is more than the level they've dragged it down to; however, those who aren't from there, such as myself, don't know the city's history. It used to be the place thousands migrated to or wanted to be. Now due to all the gang violence, people are too afraid to visit. They fear they may become the next innocent bystander, and I can't blame them. Never the less life in the Chi hasn't always been this bad; the folks there just need to remember the real power their city once had. Back in the day, many migrated to the city to escape racism but also in search of a resolution to depression.

They also went there because of all the opportunities and business that were available. Chicago has been the home and birthplace of many talented individuals; however, the movie doesn't show that it mainly showed death and the many reasons why there aren't many of us left. The picture was a sample of life there in Chiraq. It was for those who're living on the outside and don't understand how many bullets fly daily, also for those who don't understand the rate of innocent children who have been wounded or whacked. The picture helped to enlighten us all on how we've also somewhat been our own enemies and how we've contributed to the pain we carry. The film showed how we often are acting like we don't have fucking common sense at all, complaining, doing wrong, and blaming all of our problems on everyone but ourselves. It showed how some of us are out here, acting like a bunch of savages with no type of home training showing our natural black asses. Take the case with the state versus Dwight Boone-Doty and Corey Morgan. Those two cowards lured nine-year-old Tyshawn Lee, who had been at the playground playing with some friends into an alley offering him some candy and then executed the innocent young boy. The child's father had pissed off the wrong people obviously, and his son had to pay retribution. The two assailants are some stone-cold killers. No mercy was shown to that little kid before he took his last breath. They shot him in the back, in his forearm, and also in his face. The heartless bastards even shot part of his thumb off then bragged about killing him after being arrested. As if they hadn't already said and done enough, the two of them even had the nerve to say they wish they had gone back to the park and killed more kids. Mind you; he had already just shot and killed another individual the day before killing the young lady immediately and injuring the other passenger. Dwight shot the poor girl just because she had dreadlocks, and he thought she resembled some rival gang member. Little mama lost her life because of mistaken identity. Damn shame, I tell you. Have two lives gone, and for what, because of a stupid ass feud between ranking members of the Gangster Disciples? What happened to the rules and laws I thought the organizations were supposed to live by? The original gangsters said no women or kids if you choose to do otherwise nine times out of ten, you could be the next person to end up dead. They used not to play that, but now everyone is above the law, breaking all the rules and making new ones of their own. I don't believe any of them are truly living by the code of the streets. It's obvious hadn't that been the case, or they wouldn't be out here putting one another into a permanent sleep. The two gang members had planned to kill the young boy's grandmother at first but choose him instead to really hit his father, where it hurt for putting their brother Tracy Morgan down in the dirt. Retaliation at its best. Shit is crazy in these streets, and social media just adds sparks to feuds between gang members and also your regular joe. This shit has to stop; it doesn't make any sense. Jim Crow set the plan in motion to divide us; yes, this is very true, but we've also divided ourselves. If our lives matter when the police shoot us down, it should also matter on the South and West sides when the ones we care for are being taken away due to our own hands. I feel the same rules should apply to each and every one of us on every block and in every hood when we destroy ourselves and are up to no damn good. In 2001 2,349 Americans died in Afghanistan, and between 2003 to 2011, 4,424 people died in Iraq; however, with the large numbers of bodies that dropped in those two places, it still doesn't compare to how many times the grim reaper has appeared there in Chiraq. The deaths in Illinois surpasses the death toll of special forces. I'm saddened by the facts but not in disbelief.

I just find myself hurt even more because I know the individuals there who live in fear and really want better have yet to find relief. Chicago has had more murders in the past eight months of this year than all of 2015. 2,843 people have been shot across the windy city thus far, 2,327 shootings have occurred throughout all of last year. The murder rate has increased drastically. 485 people have been murdered thus far, and the year isn't even over yet. It's absurd and fucking sad that 3896 people have become shooting victims. The police had only solved twenty-four percent of the 472 homicides in 2015; that's a major difference in how many lives that have been lost or changed drastically. It's a danger zone for many it really isn't safe to leave your home. It isn't safe for the children, and it isn't safe for those who are grown. As of this morning, 2,848 shootings have occurred out of those shot 430 were actually killed by the massive gunfire. If shit doesn't change, I can only imagine how much higher the murder rate will be by the time the new year arrives. The city of Chicago has seen more murders than New York and Los Angeles put together despite the numbers of bodies that have dropped in both places despite the fact that Chi-town has fewer people. I remember the bloody fourth of July weekend in 2015 that left 55 people shot. Death comes in huge numbers to the communities living there on the regular, and seeing or hearing bullets fly has become the new normal. They're struggling with unemployment and a lack of mental health care. They need more people to step up and actually be there. Rev. Michael Pflieger (A Prominent Priest and Community Activist) lends out a helping hand a lot to the residences of the Southside although he's white, I can honestly say he does the best he can going out of his way to make a difference even though it may include him having to sacrifice his own life at times. The reverend many other pillars of the communities, and also celebrities are trying the best they can to help those in need and face the ongoing problem at hand. With all that, they try to do; however, it's still not enough. Hopelessness and desperation are weighing heavily on the people of the neighborhoods who've been hit the hardest by mass shootings and homicides. The thousands of uncalled deaths and unrest have taken a major toll on the young and the old. I really don't believe the people living there can take much more. 4300 guns have been taken off the streets, and 1530 gun arrests have been made, but that hasn't made much difference either, nor does it compare to all the lives that have been affected or slain. Bloody July will definitely be one everybody will remember, and let's not forget about all the bodies that fell in June and unforgettable September. June 18th, a sixteen-year-old boy, was shot dead just blocks away from where police officers had just spoken about a crackdown on all the gun violence and mayhem in the city. June 16th and 18th, six more people were murdered. June 19th, a three-year-old toddler named Devin Quim was shot while riding with his father to pick his mom up on "Mother's Day" luckily, he survived, but the poor young fella will be paralyzed for the rest of his life, and the shit just started. June 23rd, Jessica Hampton was stabbed to death while riding on the Red line the assailants gut her open like a piece of fish. The victim's family found out about her unfortunate death on Facebook after viewing gruesome videos of her being killed the killers made sure to broadcast the entire murder live. June 28th, another toddler named Kavan Collins, age four, was shot playing outside in the front yard of his own home; his family thought the bullets were fireworks when they heard the sounds of gunshots being let off. It was the holiday never once did they ever imagine something like that would happen even though having to reside there, they've already pretty much grown used to the gun clapping. The mysterious month of May left at least 64 people dead. In February 187 people were shot up. In January, just as the damn year was getting started, 42 people were killed, and 210 others were wounded or hurt in some way. In the month of April, the gangs continued to act a fool; 222 shootings occurred, and Angel Ortiz was shot dead for kicking a man out of the club. He was just doing his job and ended up losing his life. All this bloodshed isn't cool, just thinking about how many people have died in Chicago alone this year thus far brings me a lot of strife. Way too many are gone way too soon thanks to bullets or a knife. So many people now dead and gone behind some dumb shit gang violence or family members who couldn't seem to get along. These current acts of genocide are sickening. I shed a tear for every person who had to bury a family member this year. I understand their pain; I'm no stranger to death. Living here in Baltimore, I'm going through the same similar bullshit myself. We need to change all this madness before one day we look up, and it isn't really none of us left. Before the white man, law enforcement, or government can bring about change, we have to work harder to change ourselves first. It's hard being a black man, yes, but it's even harder for black women, many of whom are raising children on their own. It's hard for them to raise a young black boy without a strong positive male role model in the home; however, many still get the job done successfully. So many of these young and older guys are caught up though way beyond recognition due to the lack of fathers not being present and fucked up living conditions. Improper influences peer pressure and hardships have pushed most of them to the point where they just don't give a fuck. Many only have so-called gangs and other negative influences to look up too. They have no family, or a house filled with love discipline and care to come home too. The sorry ass government has made it very hard for many of them to be more than what they've settled for. The government is also in the pocket of the National Gun Association, and together, they eagerly give and sell death to all of our communities but not the suburbs. The chances of liquor stores and illegal guns crowding their streets or destroying their homes are probably never. They don't put that shit in their neighborhoods because they feel they are better, plus they want us to destroy ourselves and each other. They enjoy seeing us kill our own brothers. They enjoy kidnapping and raping our sisters. They enjoy supplying us with the drugs to sell death to our own kids or mothers. I pray for us, but I pray really hard for our youth and troubled black men. They want better, but with the lack of opportunities, room for advancement, and other options, they're left stuck in the jungle surviving the best way they think they can. These cold streets have raised a lot of women and men. I sit on the outside, praying and wondering what the fuck happened. Where did it all go wrong? Why it's so hard for us to prosper or get along? Chicago is the largest city in the United States, but it's also the most segregated. Segregation never stopped; they just sugar-coated shit in hopes that we're too stupid to notice. Our minds so clouded by their drugs that we just forgot. Many of the black populations live mostly on the Southside, which is also where the majority of the violence within the community often happens. It's like they put them in a trap to set them up to kill each other and for failure. Just like they supply us with drugs and guns tearing families apart, helping Jim Crow continue to see his dream still being fulfilled from the mass incarceration and murder rate. Over two thousand and a half residents have been shot in Chiraq, and most of them were black; this is not my assumption but a known fact. That's fucking ridiculous, just like Laquan McDonald being shot sixteen times. For what, just to show the next person that you go hard and that you're about that life or to show them that you're real? Killing for nothing, especially kids doesn't earn your stripes or street cred. Nor does taking another life make you intelligent, a gangster, or a person with skills, but changing one's self does. Instead of continuing to spread all of this hate around, we all need to try spreading more love. Melissa Boyd- Stanley, Hadiya Pendleton (Who Was an Honor Student Who Even Had A Special Visit At The White House), Pierre

Lowry, Tyjuan Pondexter (Who Was Killed Not Too Far From The Chicago Home Of President Barack Obama), Kanari Gentry-Bowers, Lavontay White, Takiya Holmes, and many others because there have been over 300 children killed in Chicago each and every one of them all gone way too soon. Gone because somebody was careless shooting like a wild cowboy in the west acting like he invincible but really just a heartless goon. Or should I say damn fool? My soul cries out for every child's life that has been lost; those innocent babies deserved more. What the hell happened to compassion? I know bullets don't have a name, but all these youth being slaughtered behind some dumb shit is a damn shame. I don't care who has a problem with my opinion. The way these savages are out here conducting themselves and living is wrong. I speak for the survivors. I speak for the parents and the unheard voices of the children who're now gone. These gangs are starting to be worse than Adolf Hitler and Saddam Hussein combined together. The tale of two cities is a sad story. Life for the folk's downtown is much safer and completely different from the families living on the Southside. They're really not affected by the double-digit unemployment, the poorly funded and underperforming schools, the abandoned buildings, and communities that look like a third world country.

They're not concerned about the proliferation of guns or the lack of opportunities and economic development. They don't care about their daily struggles or the mother who has to bury a child damn near every week. They don't care about the guns, the drugs, and the violence that has taken the lives of numerous innocent people and forcefully control the cities' deadly streets. They just don't care because at the end of the night or the beginning of the day their asses don't have to live there. I care, and so do some of the honest cops, but the distrust that has been placed in them stops individuals from coming to them for help and protection. The dirty cops have given them all a bad name. Nowadays, they're all viewed as one and the same, just like they view us blacks. However, communication and cooperation between law enforcement and the community seriously need to be addressed. Personally, I feel they all could and need to make a drastic change. The police are mad about the negative response they receive from the community. The people are mad about injustice and constant brutality. I'm bothered by all this bullshit. Everything that has been going on worldwide, not just in the city of Chicago or mine, has affected us all greatly in one way or another. All I can keep thinking about was Labor Day weekend when nine people died in a fourteen-hour span. Can you believe 92 murders throughout all of August? The Southside is the most plagued by death and gun violence. NBA star Dewayne Wade's cousin was killed less than a day after he had joined in a discussion on violence plaguing and destroying the city, his city. Wade is from Chi-town, and to see all the tragedy there bothers him too. This isn't just an ordeal he and many others feel like it shouldn't be looked over. The lives and well-being of the people there still matter even though he doesn't personally reside on the Southside. Money didn't change him, nor did city limits. His cousin Nykea Aldridge was shot and killed while pushing her baby down the street in a stroller by stray bullets. It's a crying shame that you can't even go outside for a breath of fresh air without risking your last one being taken away. It's a shame your kids have to be held hostage because it's not safe for them to go outside to play. The bullets that the gangs recklessly spray is the leading cause of many parents and children being taken away. This world we live in is cold, but it's also has gotten out of control, and people have gone crazy beyond recognition. I'm not saying this to tear us further down. I'm saying it because these problems need to be resolved now, not later. It shouldn't take a thousand more bodies to hit the paper or news before those who hold power to make a difference step in and do what's right. I'm one hundred percent for all my people, but that's doesn't mean I'm not going to speak on the fact of how we've afflicted unnecessary stress and pain upon ourselves and each other. I've always been the type of person who stood for the people; I'm just trying to speak on some truthful shit that I feel must be addressed immediately. A serious change needs to happen right now, I'm just trying to play my part doing my share or whatever I can to make sure that we're also treating one another equally. I desire to make a difference rather than discourage or destroy. I'm very honored to be a part of the "Black Lives Matter," and We Shall Not Be Moved "movement. This world is fucked up, and it needs a lot of improvement. I'm willing to die for something rather than see us hurt each other over really nothing. We've been treated unjustly and killing one another for far too long. Shit needs to change. The way we've been living is wrong, and we can't continue on in the same manner. We need to pick up books and put down the hammers. I've always been proud of the skin that I'm in, but after seeing Chiraq and Barbershop 3 last night it made me take an even deeper look around the world, around my hood, the packed graveyards, the battlefields in Iraq, all the memorials, candles, balloons, teddy bears, and cards left behind after somebody's child's blood has been washed away crossed out by chalk and a yellow police tapeline. It made me look deeper into my family values also into my real and false friends. Deeper into my relationship with my higher power and an even deeper look within. After all the thinking, I became drained but also, in some ways, afraid. Scared why? Because the entire world is living in sin in some form or fashion and I know if we aren't quick to change our wicked ways, we will all surely be condemned. I'm concerned about the troubles in many homes that are broken in the Chi but also the rest of the world. I'm concerned about decisions recklessly made in the white house and all the lives that have been lost, many at such an unfortunate cost. I'm concerned about many current events that have transpired, not just all the deaths but the lack of proper medical needs and the millions of people who're unemployed or have been fired. The state of this nation's period has me very concerned. They're the main reason I write this book.

We, the people, need a change, but most importantly, we need to change ourselves. This world has become too heartless, too cold, too dirty, too fearless, and some too bold. This world is too selfish, inconsiderate, needy, and too many who's fucking greedy. Enough is never enough; why you think they stay placing us in cuffs? Why do you think most problems in the United States mainly affect only us those who're struggling to live a life that's always been rough? We need to learn to inspire and uplift one another instead of us only being concerned with our own family members, lovers, friends, single parents, lost kids, and our praying grandmothers. Although most of us will never admit it, to survive in this land and prosper, we all need each other. Shit really fucked with my emotions when they showed the part of the movie of an innocent little girl being shot down dead on arrival soon as her lifeless body hit the ground due to some dumb gang violence. Just like Jennifer Hudson, who plays the role of the grieving mother of the child who had been slain, I too felt agonizing pain. To keep it one hundred, I was damn near in tears. It took every ounce of strength in me not to cry. It was a sad sight to see the child and her mom in such a great state of pain and the onlookers just standing there, not caring. To me, they never really do until it's one of their own laying there. Although it was just a movie, I found myself seriously bothered by the situation because the picture portrayed life in the chi for real, though they were just acting, it was mostly true. I don't want to come off as a big cry baby, but I can't lie. I think it hit so close to home because I know they're really a lot of children and adults resting up in the sky behind some bullshit they got caught up in like simply crossing the street, playing in the park, walking in the church doors, driving down the road, and be hit by a stray bullet or worse. It hit close to home because I've been a living witness to so many good young individuals being placed in a hearse. Innocent people dead because they looked at somebody wrong because of some lyrics or punchlines used in a song because of the new Jordan's they wore or because they refuse to give up their body or profit. They act a fool these days, sometimes sadly murdering each other for no damn reason at all and taking a baby or elderly person's life over fucking nothing. They have to be heartless with no conscience because it's no way I could sit around and just watch or contribute to my people suffering and not feel something. Killing another black man or woman just because they wanted the crew to think they were tough, the one in charge, and not about no bluffing. I could see if they were actually out killing for a good cause or actually fighting for something that mattered, and they deserved applause. Over five thousand deaths combined between the past two years doesn't make any sense to me or obviously the creators of the two new films I mentioned. Somebody has got to sit these hard-headed kids and gang members down somehow gathered together so they can listen. Listen to that to all the unheard voices and all the unheard cries that are left behind due to some wild shooting. It's time to put the killing on suspension and also time for all the deaf ears to pay attention. The murder and poverty issue in Chicago are not a joke. There are plenty of folks who live there that are beyond tired of the violence that's continuously putting their loved ones down in the dirt. Just like we're hurting here in Maryland, they're also going through it. The windy city will soon no longer be if people can't learn to put down the guns and bring hope and love back to the homes of so many. Chiraq is just a movie, but the concept, outlook, and messages are very real and something that most people, especially those who are black, can relate to or feel. All the bad things that took place in that particular setting is also occurring every day in so many other cities and states with no remorse. Trauma and Death are everywhere, collecting souls in huge numbers. People are dying daily; it doesn't have to be hot in the summer. Philadelphia, Florida, New York, New Jersey, Maryland, Detroit, New Orleans, Tennessee, Georgia, DC, and many other areas are also plagued by gun violence, domestic violence, and addiction to all types of drugs.

Citizens residing there are also living life every day below the poverty line full of hate, anger, frustration, and resentment while the rest struggle to have a roof over their heads. Massive piles of unpaid bills laid across the table, but barely any food to eat sometimes scraps are what they're made to provide for their family plates. We're being plucked off one by one in every area code it seems by the law and also by our own hands. I often wonder when it will stop? Will it continue on until millions of more people are lost? When will they put stricter bans on guns? When will they see we must stick together? We have enough folks already out here shooting us down for fun? The end of the year is nearing, and 2017 is right around the corner, but there's still no resolution. The politicians act oblivious to all the wounded survivors like they just ignore all the shootings. **I'm not...**

Chapter Ten

"Addiction"
Xanax, Percocet, Vicodin, Molly, and Ecstasy...

Pill popping has become an epidemic. The strong addiction that people have to it happened so fast that personally, I'm still trying to figure out exactly how and why it happened. I mean, I have a few ideas, but I'm not sure of the exact cause. What I do know is the addicts who're strung out on the shit are putting more of that in the system than Bobby Brown's history, which was daily intakes of large amounts of heroin and that pure cocaine. Drugs have destroyed many lives homes and families; it also destroyed their brains. Still, every type is a trend when it comes to teens and adults, but it's all highly addictive and deadly. The medication has young kids and old heads running around here, acting like they're mentally disabled or terminally ill. They're doing whatever to receive that special feeling stealing lying doing whatever to get that next fix or pill. Not once do I think they've ever thought about how many people it has killed. Whitney Houston, the late great singer, actress, producer, model, and mother, were found dead at the age of just 48. She didn't get to live as long as she probably could have due to putting that shit up her nose. I love her to death, and there will never be another; don't get me wrong, but at the same time, I want to speak on some of her dirty laundry that got exposed. I do not know for certain if she had a thing for prescription pills, but she did have a serious addiction to drugs in general, which ultimately ended up getting the best of her. I wish she could have received the proper helped she needed in time. I wish she'd been able to get rid of the people she didn't need. Had those things happened, she may have been around to save her only seed possibly. Her baby girl Kristina died too almost the same way, and their deaths are some of the reasons why I'm trying to bring awareness to this ongoing problem today. Millions of individuals around the world are somewhere running a scam on a doctor for a prescription for medicine that they don't really need. Whereas those who are really sick and in need are being denied proper medication or treatment. Not to shade anyone, I realize it's a problem. I'm merely just shedding light that "Junkies" like them make it extremely hard for everybody else. The statement one bad apple spoils the brunch is true. Others are highly affected by the bullshit that they try to do. Michael Jackson, age 50, the king, singer, songwriter, record producer, dancer, actor, and philanthropist, is another great legend who's dead because a fake doctor prescribed too much medicine to help him cover up the demons in his head. The entire world cried when he and Mrs. Houston died, but the media didn't let their addictions slide. They enjoy advertising other people's mess. They broadcasted so much negativity after their bodies were found that their souls probably couldn't even rest. They showed no remorse to the family members that were left behind. Why do you think little Kristina also lost her mind? I feel so sorry for her, and I blame the parents and the world who criticized them daily, making it extra hard for that already troubled girl. Prince, the legendary singer-songwriter multi-instrumentalist, and record producer dead at the age of 57 due to fentanyl opioid overdose. He was popping pill after pill until it left him literally eternally coma toast. Heath Ledger also died due to accidental overdose of several medications, including pain killers, sleeping pills, and anti-anxiety drugs. He was an extraordinary actor, but now he is dead because his addiction ended up growing stronger and stronger. There are so many people I could name of all ages, but there's no need because by now, I should have made my point that popping or snorting pills do kill. Nobody is exempt; it doesn't matter who you are. That shit is deadly, yet they use it to get what they consider a good feel. Don't they understand the consequences are real? So, is cardiac arrest and a stroke. They spend tons of money on Oxycodone, Methadone, and Hydrocodone, and those drugs sell just as much if not more than that boy or Coke. Back in the year of 2014, over 47,000 people died from an overdose of either pharmaceutical opioid analgesics or heroin. In the year 2015, the overdose death rate surpassed 50,000; it's continued to increase this year, yet politicians don't see a problem with shit like this. They see nothing wrong with it damn near being at least one to three addicts in every home. This issue is just as bad as the crack epidemic when it first hit. People were ill and looking for any way to get it. Many act like they can't go a single day without it. God forbid there's a shortage, a denial from a doctor, or a sudden drought. Depression, stressing, and many other reasons why thousands of people have chosen this as a mechanism to cope. I don't think they understand popping pills is just as highly addictive as if they were snorting or shooting up dope. The elderly, middle-aged, and teens are all suffering from the addiction, although most of them refuse to admit it. The younger ones think it's cool; it's as if they are willing to play the fool and follow what the crowd is doing. Peer pressure blinds them to the things and people that eventually will be their ruin if they don't stop. Even worse, they could die. Taking medication that isn't prescribed to you or with alcohol is just as dangerous as when people speedball. Those pills can also make your heart pop or make your lungs drop. The body can be severely damaged by the abuse causing failure to the kidneys, liver, and other organs. Physical dependence could become a problem due to high tolerance to the medication and the need to always wanting more and more. Withdrawal can be deadly or at least make you wish you were. I hear the side effects are no joke. I've seen dope fiends balled up like a baby, hurting and unable to eat, sleep, or think because they need another fix. Some loved ones have even contributed to the bad habits out of fear of what they may go out and do for it or because they're extremely sick. We sometimes do crazy shit for those we care for not because we want them to get high but because we don't want them to die. It's as if we're stuck between a rock and a hard place. We don't like to see our babies having sex or doing something out the ordinary for a 10 Vicodin or 30 Percocet. We don't like to see our family or friends strung out or watch them intake drugs that we know could eventually get them hurt. I know they like their "Yellow Jackets, "Happy Pills, "and "Sleeping Pills." We know they like them all, but none of its good for them mentally or physically, and we need to try to find a way to bring a much-needed end to this ignored abuse. This is a growing problem among teens. The youth seem to use the drugs to get high to rid themselves of pain or to help with work or education. I guess they believe it gives them superpowers. They steal pills from friends and relatives.

 We have to watch it with a closer eye. They're killing themselves, and those who surround them don't even know. Hopefully, now that I've attempted to make them aware, maybe they will intervene and show the troubled adolescents that they do care. First and foremost, those adults who have a drug problem need to try to get help and be better examples for our future. Why continue to let the cancer spread? They're already killing them off enough with guns and toxic waters filled with lead. We got to go back to saying no to drugs, find better ways to cope, and put down the toxins and spread more hope, knowledge, and love. The twelve-step program, the Holy Bible, or Koran, does work if you work it. You just have to really want it for yourself...

Chapter Eleven

"2016 Is Over 2017 Is Here "
It's A New Year but Hasn't Shit Changed
But The Date...

It's a new day with new beginnings. I'm grateful because this past season was rough. Many didn't survive, and if you did, it's a blessing because what we all had to endure was very tough.

It's a new year, but sadly nothing has changed but the weather and the date. Shit is still fucked up. People are still struggling, grieving, being buried, unemployed, homeless, hopeless, don't know how they're going to pay the bills, and still scraping together funds to have some sort of meal on the plate. Bodies are still dropping; it's like they refuse to put an end to gun violence just like they refuse to stop pill-popping. The clock barely got to strike twelve before bullets started ringing through the cold night air. Mind you, 2016 ended with 762 homicides in Chicago and over 300 in Baltimore, not to mention the other states. Trump threatens if Chiraq doesn't fix the horrible ongoing problem, he will be immediately sending the Feds in. The outcome won't be good, so I'm sure they don't want that to happen. I suggest they get it together quickly before Donald sends in his goons to kill everything moving. I guess taking the gangs out will be his way of improving. Not that he really cares about all the gun violence there is. The asshole is only doing that out of spite because of the ongoing problem he has with the city's Mayor Rahm Emanuel, who formerly served for President Obama's chief of staff. He's trying to storm the city because of his personal beef. He could give two fucks for real about the innocent souls that's getting wrapped up in the white sheets. It's been 228 shootings and 42 killings there thus far. Only God knows what the body count might be tomorrow. The savages and grim reaper wasted no time reloading their weapons and hitting the already tormented communities like a street sweeper. Not even a full 24 hours into the new year before bloodshed quickly started spreading throughout the many deadly cities, including my own. As I watched the morning news and read the paper on Monday, I wasn't at all shocked to see another bloody body here on the Westside of Baltimore drop but also in other areas. The gangs have stopped tagging walls; they're obviously too busy targeting one another just to end up in an early grave, wheelchair, or hospital bed with a shit bag on, trying to recover. I thought to see Freddie die unjustly while the world said fuck us was enough to make some people want to do better. But I was wrong. I thought the aftermath of the riot was enough for the politicians to listen, but it isn't. They're still doing fucked up shit and just expect us to bow down, accept whatever, and be quiet. They spent 2.5 million on Damascus gear and hard-shell body armor for the riot, including $84,480 for next day delivery as protests escalated over Gray's death. They were prepared to make a mockery out of us. They had their guns already loaded with one in the head, anticipating the moment they could be busted then wonder why they can't be trusted. No money has been given to schools that are barely surviving, and I'm not even going to speak on the ones they allowed to be closed down. They have no money to pay the teachers either, so they claim, they've just recently taken another pay cut. They didn't have funds to aid in getting new books, but they had money to fund crooks. Trevon Green was sentenced to five years for committing arson during the riot they say they had it all on camera. The murder of Freddie was also on camera, but evidence came up missing and the prosecution must not have paid attention.

 Every officer that took part or actually committed the murder were all found not guilty and acquitted. The witnesses and friends of Freddie have been harassed and arrested for false charges because the cops felt the need to apply more pressure. One of their known tactics is to instill fear. However, the six officers all walked away, scot-free with huge smiles plastered across their faces. There has been a huge outcry here in Baltimore. The residents of our city are mad, and so am I, but as far as the outcome is concerned, I'm not that surprised. Let's be real about it. How many officers are actually being held accountable or doing time for murder or assault cases? As I said hasn't shit changed, all the foul shit we've been going through still remains the same. I thought the difficulties of 2016 would make us grind harder, not just smarter, but it's too many greedy people out there who don't know their place or are just as heartless and ruthless as Nino Brown when he took over The Carter. Too many individuals are out for self-acting like crabs in a bucket, tearing others down instead of lending some encouragement or help — too many afraid to see the next person shine. Too many stuck with a negative frame of mind. Too many spending money they really don't have — too many letting their freedom just be up for grabs. We need more motivators; we have enough miserable envious haters. We need to come to our senses, bring about peace, and learn to inspire. We already have enough opposition trying to hold us back, lock us away, or keep us higher. We need more educators and business-minded folks. We need ownership and knowledge so we can have more to call our own and so that we may be aware of our rights and keep them from being revoked. We need to buy the block back, but it's hard for some to understand the vision because they're blinded by drugs and violence that plague their cities, or they're too busy spending money on buying a new pair of shoes, an outfit, pills, or crack. Many of us have to change our mentality and the way we think. If we don't start putting ourselves first, we put ourselves at an even greater risk of becoming extinct or hurt. Donald Trump won, he's the president-elect, and there are rumors surfacing around that it's due to his Russian connections. As far as I'm concerned, we the people and the rest of this country is done. I don't respect him or acknowledge him as my President; he's a belligerent asshole for real.

 On the first day in office, he fires all Ambassadors and Special Envoys hired by Obama. He ordered them to be out of the office by inauguration day. On the day of the actual inauguration, he signed an executive order instructing the agencies to minimize the cost of the affordable care act. His racist team hung a portrait of former President Andrew Jackson on the wall in the oval office (that's

Trump American idol besides Bush). Keep in mind Jackson is remembered best for signing the Indian Removal Act of 1830, which eventually forced Native Americans to relocate. The sudden need to migrate resulted in what we call the "Trail of Tears" that left more than 4,000 dead. Jackson is also the same president who introduced the Spoils System under which new administration purge the civil service, packing it with their own personal supporters. If the public has been paying attention, that's exactly what Donald Dumb has been doing every appearance he makes now, and during the campaign, he stages all the front row areas with his stupid supporters to ensure applause and to make it look extra good for the public. He'll be fronting for the camera as people do for Instagram. Not only is he an unethical liar, but he's a womanizer and a con, and he's showing us the extent he will go to fulfill his prejudice ways.

 He treats women like animals and personal slaves. He has no respect or regard for us females or human life in general. Trump is a fucking animal, and it's reasons like the ones I'm about to mention that makes me really not like him. The pervert signed an order reintroducing a Ronald Reagan era gag policy, which prevents federal funding from going toward any international organizations that offer or promote abortions. This policy will have a great impact on women only. The lack of money will prevent them from being able to provide services many females need, such as contraception, family planning, or health advice. As a result of this, women are at an even higher risk of severe health problems and death. If doing trifling shit like that isn't bad enough, he's resurrecting plans for two new oil pipelines which had previously been rejected by the Obama administration. Reckless moves such as this further let us know that he doesn't care about global warming or anything else that's really of importance. It's been 70- and 80-degree weather in January and February, which isn't normal, yet he continues to discuss his businesses and his damn self. Donald has even signed an executive order for the immediate construction of his great wall of hate between the U.S. and Mexico border separating parents from their children. That same order also included the Department of Homeland security to publish weekly lists of crimes committed by immigrants.

The new President of this country is seriously devilish, on his best bullshit and unethical. His intentions are evil, he is beyond dishonest and wicked. I don't support or believe in what he's doing. I have morals, and to me, what he's doing is just another form of modern-day segregation. I'm terrified about the repercussions of his decisions. I'm terrified about what is bound to come. Another order that he signed the same day blocks the government from offering visas to anyone visiting from Syria, Iraq, Iran, Libya, Somalia, Sudan, and Yemen. He's also temporarily blocking refugees from entering the country except for those who've fled Syria; they will be banned indefinitely. I guess he kept the promise he made during the campaigns when he threatened to place a ban on Muslim immigration. Trump is the devil in disguise, but he has the nerve to be out here trying to play God. He wants to reinstate the "Black Site" prisons ran by the CIA that often uses enhanced interrogation techniques such as waterboarding torture. This motherfucker is Satan in the physical form, and all his followers who go out their way to support him are his advocates. If you're not white or American, you are standing in great danger. Real talk. Our lives are no safer here than a complete foreign stranger. If Donald isn't impeached or killed first, he's about to take us back to the old days when they deliberately went out of their way to make people of any color that isn't theirs lives a living hell. That so-called President doesn't give a damn about the wellbeing of this country or certain people that reside in or outside of it. Living in fear has become the circumstance for many who's skin isn't pale. I'm very afraid right now because the White House has definitely become the foundation where all the racists' rednecks' dwell. With him, in charge, there probably won't be any peace, justice, reforms, advancements, affordable homes, or food and, of course, no schools or bail. If we didn't have our shit together before, we must do so now because you're in a world of trouble constantly when you refuse to bow down. With his racist ass in the office, I can see us all doomed. He's already making fucked up decisions that could leave a lot of us taxpayers' money and lives consumed. We the people didn't vote for his arrogant, ignorant ass, he won due to questionable electoral votes. I swore when they said the results of the election I damn near choked. I'm black, so I'm very concerned with him running shit. It's possible all of our rights that people have and still are fighting for could be revoked. I cried all day long just as many others around the world did because putting Trump in the White House, might as well have put a trigger to our own heads. Shit, the Muslims aren't the only individuals he has threatened to fill up with lead. He hasn't even been in that chair for six months, and he's already making poor decisions that could cost us dearly. When I say cost us dearly, I'm not just speaking of the coins that we make yearly either, I'm speaking on things that many of us often take for granted. I pray Jesus can continue to be a fence around this country, not just me and mine because when it comes to the struggle and the messed up economy, trust and believe it's not only colored folks that are bound to be standing in welfare, unemployment, or food pantry line. When it comes to the way Donald Dumb, I mean Donald Trump, moves, we can all find ourselves facing more obstacles just as we can all possibly find ourselves being left behind or placed on the front lines to fight another war. I pray mostly for the poor because life is already complicated enough for them, and they don't need any extra bullshit from him. My people came too far to have to go back, but that's exactly where the elected president may try to send us. The rest of the politicians aren't going to defend or protect us. In one way or another, they all just neglect us. We must stand up for ourselves instead of just killing one another and dying for nothing. The same energy that's put into shooting someone over color, you can do the right thing and stand for something. Just because things are extra hard for us doesn't mean we should just settle or up and quit. We have to move forward regardless of the adversary and find ways to handle it. The rally and marches that's taken place in Baltimore, New York, and Washington, DC, were of great importance. I'm mad that I wasn't able to be a part of history, but I did, however, pray for our victory. That particular movement was a day where once again, we demanded justice, equality, fair pay, employment instead of entrapment, and an urgent end to the police reform and brutality without having to be busted upside our head or beaten down like dogs. That day was one where we made them have no other choice but to listen. However, that doesn't guarantee that they were all actually paying attention. It made me proud to see us come together again as one during MLK weekend and the marches for our women. I just wish we could learn to come together on the regular instead of at special events such as those or when something else bad happens. I say that because some people only talk a good game like those who had so much to say on the internet and so forth in regard to who was running for president but didn't get off their ass or computer and go out and vote. Many complain, but not as many try to do what we have to in order to bring about change. Most look at all this shit as a joke or game, but it's nothing funny about being killed unjustly or falsely detained. Nothing that we black folks have had to endure last year or the many years before is a laughing matter. I shed tears daily for every life that was taken and for every home that has now been shattered. I cried for the hopeless and all the ones who've been bound by depression and grief or just battered. I feel for us who survived the madness and are still moving on. Crazy world. I know God couldn't have had all the nonsense and all this mess in mind on the day he created it no more than I wanted to be terrified after watching Maliki or the other demonic creepy kids in the movie "The Children of The Corn ". I don't believe many of the parents of the so-called gangsters wanted that lifestyle for their kids. They had to have wanted more, but it's obvious those individuals had other plans for their lives in store. The devil loves to capitalize and prey on the minds of the weary and the weak. He stays on a mission to build a strong army of his own to roam the streets. The devil doesn't have a love for anybody either. He really doesn't care if you have money, a big home, an expensive car, and all your shit allegedly on fleek or all together. His only desire, similar to Jim Crow, is to conquer, divide, and then destroy. I believe he anxiously awaits the moment when he can recruit a new soul to be his personal toy. Many of us have gained the world but sold our souls for prices that haven't always come cheap. To him, it doesn't matter as long as he can cause chaos and confusion. Reminds me a lot of our former presidents and the soon to be one as well. Trump is bound to have us locked in a cage or free but still feeling like we're living in a cell or hell. For anybody to believe him or the devil has good intentions, they must be crazy also delusional. They both can be very persuasive, look at how Trump played Hillary, and let's not forget how the devil convinced Eve to take the apple and bite it. They both are something slick, and many are going to fall victim to the manipulative bullshit. This I get, but we don't have to continue to settle or take the bait just because of it. We have to get it together this year before we find ourselves not just being shot down but back in shackles on a ship getting deported. To hell with the self-inflicted genocide. We need to unite as one, empowering ourselves and the movement even if the racist whites and government don't approve of it. Our lives do matter; they have value and still hold value. American politicians, law enforcement, and other government officials make a choice not to see but that doesn't mean when to have to be blind as well. They aren't oblivious to the death, drugs, or destruction they single-handedly orchestrated or created. They simply don't care, so we must. **It's Time…**

Chapter Twelve

"SEX TOYS"

Human Trafficking Is Just Another Form of Modern-Day Slavery...

Sex Tourism is a billion-dollar industry that encourages the exploitation of women and little girls. They're marketed specifically for common ass pedophiles who prey on the young or have sick thoughts that having sex with adolescents will rid the demons the keep inside or cure a sexually transmitted disease. Sick bastard please. That's beyond insane. I couldn't believe something such as this existed, but it does, I'm appalled, this business is not only downright degrading it's disgusting and exactly why when it comes to the safety of children, I've never been very trusting. I watch everybody; family members included they're not exempt. Some of my friends have told me secrets about perverted bastards just like them. I've also been abused myself, so I definitely take the specific matter personally. In my eyes, no real man or woman would ever or should ever do such a thing. They have no idea the open wounds and scars that they often leave behind. Trafficking is also a billion-dollar industry 32 to be exact. For those who may be unaware of what that is, I will gladly educate you. Trafficking involves the transportation or trade of human beings for the prime purpose of work or sex, if not both. There are over 2.5 million people worldwide who are ensnared in trafficking at any given time and at any given place. No one is safe, especially women and girls. I've learned that human trafficking can have an impact on every race and background. People from all different aspects of life are trafficked, and for many different reasons. Men are purchased for the hardest jobs, children for labor positions in textile, agriculture, diamonds, and the fishing industry. Women and our baby girls are most times kidnapped becoming either traded or sold into the commercial sex industry, which includes prostitution and other forms of sexual exploitation. Not all slaves are taken unwillingly; however, all of them are victims of modern-day slavery. I pray God has mercy on whoever's soul that came up with this bright idea. Human trafficking is the worst form because it's detrimental to the well-being of those individuals. It deliberately separates the victims from all that they know; people, places, and things. The mental and physical torture eventually leaves those females completely isolated, feeling alone, and abandoned. Nine times out of ten, the average victim doesn't speak the language of her captors or fellow victims. Each year there are over 800,000 women and children who're transported or traded across international borders while some are being trafficked within countries. Over 64,000 African American women are missing, and we still don't know exactly what happened to our six girls that just up and disappeared. We still need and want them back, and none of them have been forgotten at least I haven't. Sex trafficking is another major problem within the U.S. that has also been neglected. It remains to be unseen outside of pornography and prostitution most times because it operates out of unmarked brothels in unsuspecting suburban neighborhoods. They also operate out of private and public establishments like strip clubs, massage parlors, and spas. Law enforcement is aware of this because their asses were a part of the perverted party. Men and boys are rarely attacked because they're often the ones trying to put all these people on their back or the track. Women and little girls have been preyed upon the most. They make up the largest category of sex trafficking victims, and they're apprehending their next prey in the most unthinkable places. Shit, truth be told, the predators are everywhere, but they normally migrate from the east to the west. However, victims sometimes are trafficked from one country to another, and that's at any given moment. VICTIMS EXIST EVERYWHERE LET ME MAKE THAT CLEAR IF I ALREADY HAVEN'T. The most affected areas are the poorest and from the most unstable countries. Human trafficking and impoverishment are common factors amongst the victims. Cowards love to prey on the weak; you can tell by the way they conduct themselves and speak. The struggle for many of those women and girls is real, which has undermined their income, self-esteem, and economic position. I blame the perverts, and I blame the crime lords for this nonsense. They sell souls eagerly just for a quick profit. The shit is unjust and degrading, and the government should make them stop. That probably will never happen because it seems they support the self-proclaimed pimps, sugar daddies, and johns. They all have lost their rabbit ass mind. The sex business pays off dearly if you base it off the number, but it's also wrong and cruel. Those animals kidnap, torture, kill, and rape. They make seven-year-old girls pop pussy for a fat French fuck, and they make them sniff lines for a Russian guy off a serving plate. They're responsible for the epidemic of international human trafficking, sex trafficking, physical & mental abuse, and prostitution, which is supposed to be illegal in most states. How the captors treat the female victims eventually causes a severe effect on their physical, mental, and emotional well-being. All the stress, grief, fear, distrust, forced addiction, and suicidal thoughts take a toll. I admire those who get the strength to fight back because it has to take a lot to survive some tragic shit like that. Many of them end up turning to alcohol and drugs on their own just to be able to cope with the pain. Can you blame them having to endure what they have had to? It would probably drive anybody insane. Sex trafficking is deadly and also a danger to public health and ourselves. It erodes the government while the authority is encouraging the widespread of women and children to continue to be sexually violated. It also threatened the security of all the many vulnerable populations around the world.

 The same criminals who're involved in drugs and guns on a larger scale then these petty so-called dope dealers. They're also the same people who are selling and buying ass. Donald Trump has spoken on a lot of things, but I've never heard that be one. His ass probably supports what they do though he's probably been up in one of the brothels having his own fun. As a matter of fact, I know he was putting minors on their back ask Ghislaine Maxwell. He demanded Chicago put down the gun, he said nothing about the men who're mostly from Asia, the United States, and Western Europe stealing human bodies and selling them on the market like a piece of candy or a cinnamon bun. With the current president being an unethical womanizer himself, I can foresee this issue getting further out of hand. We're already living in a society where females are undervalued or simply not valued at all. Nothing has changed all these years, and in most men's eyes, that's the law. Their ignorant ways place a female at a greater risk of being abused, trafficked, or coerced into sexual slavery. I pray that the Lord can cover as many of us as he can. If we leave it up to those cold-hearted snakes, there's no telling what might happen. They will continue to try and tear us down physically and spiritually if we don't wise up, educate ourselves, be more mindful of the company we keep, and learn to value our own. We have to protect ourselves because it's been made clear to us time and time again that we can't really rely on anybody else. We've had to guard our daughters and continuously let them know that they're important, beautiful, loved, smart, they have family and friends that really care. People like Shandra Woworuntu and so many other victims wish that they had honest people around that actually cared. Ms. Woworuntu was also a victim, but glory is to God; she was able to survive and get free. I'm thankful because look at how many other people there are that haven't been so fortunate. Ladies, please be careful because everything I just said is true. Don't be stupid because this can also happen to your loved ones, friends, strangers, or even worse you...

Chapter Thirteen

"PRAYING FOR THIS CRAZY WORLD"
God Is Willing He Is Able He Always Understands...

I pray we can focus more on raising intelligent, respectful, honest, hardworking, determined, and responsible young girls and boys. I want them to know that they're smart kings and queens who can be anything their hearts desire. Instead of being focused on making the cut on the next reality show, being a forty-year-old dope boy, being a stripper, a bad bitch, molding a thot or baby gangster who probably can't even spell correctly. Let alone value themselves, respect others, want something out of life, active in sports, love to educate his or her mind, or want to be the next master chef junior. We are more than what they've labeled or tried to make us out to be. We just have to rid ourselves of all the negativity. Many of us idealize the wrong things, not realizing having those things will never make you, and those white people who believe they're our higher power, equal one of the same. I pray we stop being concerned about who the next person is sleeping with, especially when we're out fornicating ourselves. Stop being worried about what other people have. We are more than that, and we have so much more to really be worried about. There's a lot going on worldwide, and the people are oblivious to it as if those situations can't somehow affect them and have us also going directly through it. I pray we can change the negative mentality we sometimes have. Being the trending topic means nothing compared to all the important matters that now lay at stake. Instead of trying to pose for Instagram or Facebook, we need to humble ourselves. I pray that God can help us all out before it's too late. Me personally, I don't want to continue to see all the drugs and guns the government ships into our neighborhoods or gangs and fakes gods to keep controlling our fate. I know you stay busy because there's so many who are calling on you, but we need you right away. Three more people were killed and sixteen wounded during the first six hours of the new year. Four people were killed, and twenty-five others were wounded in separate shootings. How can one be full of cheer? Enough is enough! I don't know how much longer we can wait. The struggle and crime are already steadily climbing at a high fast rate. I need you to send food for the hungry, a shelter for the homeless, hope for the hopeless, and love for the heartless. Everything you think we need really. I seriously want and wish to see everybody safe and eating, not just me and mine straight. God, I desire to see all your children prosper and grow. When I pray unto you as I am today, I do it for us all, not just for the ones I love or know. The world is in shambles, and it's time for the gangs to put down the hammers. We do things we shouldn't often, and we buy shit that we don't need just to impress the next person who could really care less if you're doing bad or good. To them, most times, you don't even exist or matter. I guess many have forgotten that the ultimate objective was to free ourselves and people from the hood. The change that we all claim we want to see is also the exact same change we must all take part in and be. We need to build and uplift our communities. We can't continue only to be focused on ourselves or our own family. We have to take a stand and make a difference while we still have a chance. The revolution wasn't going to change just because a black man sat in that high chair. Shit, you see how people are still struggling even more because of Obama Care. No shade. I'm just telling you how it really is. I got love for my president, but sometimes I have also to question his way of doing things and how he's often handled his biz. There have been many moves made and sat-downs that I personally don't approve of, and I'm not talking about the private conversations between him and Queen Liz. When it comes to my opinion of the current or former presidents of this country, it is what it is. It's not like I'm telling lies or leaking important material to spies. God, the decisions they've made or don't make has a major impact on the way many people, especially those of color or less fortunate, have to live. As you can see, they've pretended to be for the people, but when it really comes down to our wellbeing, especially those living below the poverty line, they really don't have zero fucks to give. To me, all they will ever be concerned about is money, sex, oil, drugs, and a position of power. It doesn't matter to them how many people die from whatever cause they have no fucking empathy or compassion when it comes to thousands dying by the hour. They're beyond cruel and heartless when it comes to us the people. Their constant fucked up actions have left a bad taste in my mouth that's really sour. I really don't have any love or regard for those types of cowards. God, I don't respect the mindset of many of the so-called "Thugs & Animals" in Mayor Rawlings Blake's words to be exact, running around the cities filling each other with lead either. I'm tired of seeing them slaughter each other. They're armed for war camouflaged in all black shooting guns; they aren't even big enough to carry on their fucking small backs. I don't condone them putting their own neighborhoods, their own people, and their own flesh and blood under severe attack.

I'm praying hard for us all because things need to change. It hurts me a lot to see us out there, blasting pistols and machine guns off, being reckless, not concerned about the next person. It hurts to see the brain fragments on the ground or white wall. It's been so much bloodshed over the past few years that you would have thought it was a flood. It hurts me personally to keep seeing people's heads blown off or shots spread out all over, leaving the homes and streets full of blood.

I pray for peace and understanding because right now, it's hard to find or feel the love. I pray you can remove the hatred from within our hearts. Create in us a new one. It bothers me a lot to see us still falling victim to Jim Crow's racist ass wishes. I'm tired of giving him and his followers the attention they so badly want or free entertainment. They get a thrill out of seeing us drag or tear one another down. They enjoy seeing us stretched out dead filled up with bullet holes or stab wounds. I pray you can forgive me for holding grudges. It just matters like that, that I take to the heart.

Excuse my language God, but their shenanigans really get under my fucking skin. You should have seen how many of them were leaping for joy when the news reporter stated the 2015 and 2016 murder rate. Nearly seven hundred bodies, if not more, are gone and will never be seen or heard from again in the Murder land. I've attended way too many funerals, candlelight visuals, memorials, and waits. I find it very sad that I've seen more of our youth getting buried in an early grave than I've seen them dressed in cap and gown, proudly sitting patiently as their names are called to walk across the stage to graduate. It's seriously a crying damn shame, excuse my language once again. I pray our youth and some adults can get it together as soon as possible. Time is being cut shorter and shorter. Their time is now; our time is now; we may not get another chance at this. I want better for my people. I pray that they want the same for themselves. I would love to see them doing good. Bless them father please, with the knowledge, wisdom, and power to succeed. Bless them with mannerisms and values, so they don't keep getting caught up in the wrong things like greed. I pray you can bless the entire race with the strength to keep fighting this fight but also bless them with a positive mind. I pray you can teach each one of them how to use their brains as a weapon. Help them to understand we can win, but it doesn't always have to be resolved with violence, firearms, knives, or aggression. I pray you can help those who are troubled. Show them, Lord, that it's not too late to turn it around. Let them know we care and that they can be more than what so many have settled for, and that's not very much. I want better for our children. I want better for us period, but I think some of us don't view life the same. They're too caught up in the fast life, sex, fortune, material things, and fame. I pray mostly for the youth the future of this world. I pray for nothing but the best when it comes down to every young boy and girl. I pray us adults can learn to be better leaders and positive role models. I pray we can show them by leading by example. I pray we can open their eyes more so that they may be able to see there's way more to life than social sites, apps, molly, fake people, being bad bitches, that nigga turning up in the streets, doing dumb shit, staying lit, having kids too early, popping pills, and bottles or any of that other type of dumb bullshit. All that stuff means nothing to me, and it shouldn't be of that much of an importance to many others either. We, adults, need to pull ourselves together quickly. We need to change immediately. We must show these kids better ways to conduct themselves and better ways of handling life's difficult hardships and obstacles if we want to make them a believer. I pray teamwork will make the dream work.

We must live right, be honest, content, independent, responsible, hardworking, and ambitious. This will show them that with commitment, perseverance, faith, patience, and determination that they too can be successful and that they also can become prosperous achievers. We must all play our part if we want to get through all the turmoil if we want to get through all the pain, stress, and strife that we are often feeling. I pray that you send mercy but also healing. Times are getting harder, but we aren't moving smarter. We aren't doing right by our family members, our sons, and daughters. I know it's many others out there other than myself that are also tired of living in the cold or dark. God, I pray you can help us to unite together as one and not continue to drift apart. Be what we need to ignite the spark. I pray you can lay your precious hands that comfort and heal down on us and leave a mark. I don't want to continue seeing family's homes, churches, countries, friends, and minorities torn apart. We have been going through hell for way too long. It's time to get it together. I pray all these things with so much care, compassion, and love in my heart to you and your son Jesus. I pray for these things to make a difference. I pray the change I wish for is on the way because folks are losing their faith by the day. The enemy and opposition want us to stay broken. They want us beefing, acting crazy, and disturbing the peace. They want us to be shot down in the streets. They want us to suffer, but I declare victory. They want us to fold under pressure but hear me, brothers and sisters when I say that's what creates diamonds. Stay encouraged, stay strong, and continue to believe. They want to take us off focus; the system long ago was designed that way. They want to twist the word or choose everyone's choice of religion. They want us to think like an uneducated slave and bow down to them. No matter the wrongs they continue to do, I pray they'll be forgiven. I refuse to let their ignorance stop us from fully living. We all have a greater purpose, and I humbly ask you, Father, that you be merciful and help us fulfill that purpose. Your grace has always been sufficient, so I know in due time you will come through; we just have to hold on and hold out. Patience is truly a virtue. I know you're able to have our back; we just must repent, try our best to live right, and continue to give you all the praise and glory. I pray that I've educated, inspired, encouraged, and blessed someone

with this much needed story. With you, all things are possible, so I pray today for many things but mostly for change, and I'm hoping this book and prayer can be the start. I know we've fallen short and haven't always played the part, but please look out for us, God. I know you still have a huge heart. We need you like we need oxygen to breathe; if not, Trump might have as all nailed to a wall of hate or hanging from burning old oak trees...
I Want Better for Us All, But We First Must Want It For Ourselves...

Part Two Coming Very Soon...

Biography

Shamira Camper, age 36 is a Maryland native raised by her grandmother and older sibling she grew up witnessing and personally experiencing hardships, death, drugs, and poverty. Not wanting the suffering of herself or others to be in vain she decided to pour all of their pain into her books. Determined to fulfill her dreams, be a voice of reason for those who've been ignored, and a blessing to someone else. Currently she is working on her next book "Couldn't Tell Nobody but God."